RE___
to Bondage

Karen Romero

COLOSSIANS 2:14-15

ISBN 978-0-9961504-9-1
COPYRIGHT © 2018 by Karen Frazier Romero
P.O. BOX 1601 . BROUSSARD, LOUISIANA 70518

All Scripture verses are from the King James Version Bible
(Expositor's Study Bible Edition 2005)

RETURN
to Bondage

KAREN FRAZIER ROMERO

To Loula and Lorraine:
Who graciously showed me the difference between religion and a true relationship with Jesus Christ.

CONTENTS

Chapter One

RETURN TO BONDAGE

The title *Return to Bondage* may sound a bit strange, but as this book unfolds, it will become evident as to why this particular title was chosen. The front cover of this book depicts a person bound by heavy chains, with an iron padlock securing any chance of an easy escape. It is hard to imagine that anyone would voluntarily be placed in such a helpless position.

Who, in their right mind, would *want* to be in bondage? I believe that the answer to this question is *"no one."* This book was written for those who truly desire a real relationship with God and want to serve Him with all of their heart, soul and mind. There are many out there who want that special bond, but unfortunately, man-made religion has been a stumbling block; keeping them in bondage and holding them back from the freedom that God desires for us.

The word "bondage" can be defined as *"the state of being a slave."*[1] The thesaurus gives synonyms for the word "bondage" to include: *slavery, enslavement, servitude, subjugation, subjection, oppression, domination, exploitation...*[2] In the context of this manuscript, both the definition and the synonyms certainly strike a resounding chord.

---

[1] https://en.oxforddictionaries.com/definition/bondage
[2] https://en.oxforddictionaries.com/thesaurus/bondage

It is not common knowledge that *Webster's Collegiate Dictionary* traces the etymology of the word "religion" back to the old Latin word *religio* meaning *"taboo, restraint."* An even deeper study of the word reveals that "religion" is derived from the two words, *re* and *ligare. Re* is a prefix meaning *"return,"* and *ligare* means *"to bind;"*[3] in other words, "return to bondage."

It took me a moment to digest this fact when I first stumbled upon it. *Religion equals bondage?* With thousands of forms of religion in the world today, it is impossible to think that billions of humans are being enslaved by their respective religions. Could scores of people be deceived into believing that being a part of a religion will ultimately gain them an afterlife or eternal life in their version of Heaven? With so many different views and paths, which one is accurate?

This book will set out to investigate if being a part of a religion is pleasing to God, the almighty Creator of the Universe. We will examine many crucial subjects that may require you to truly evaluate your own beliefs and spiritual motives. Some questions will include: What does the Bible say about religion and religious people? Why does being a part of a religion make people feel good about themselves and their eternal standing with God? What truly pleases God? From where should we gather our beliefs? Can a person earn something from God by good works and exemplary behavior? Will devoted religious people go to Heaven upon death? Can dedicated religious people go to Hell?

Some will say that the answers to these questions will be my own opinion, but through the Scriptures found in God's Word, we will find a clear and concise answer for each and every one of these questions posed in this introduction. Once a person

---

[3] http://www.tentmaker.org/Dew/Dew1/D1-EtymologyOfReligion.html

understands God's simple plan of salvation and His willingness that no one should perish, but that all should come to the knowledge of truth, then there is no denying just how much God truly loves each and every one of us. 2 Peter 3: 9 states, **"The Lord is not slack concerning His promise, as some men count slackness; but is long-suffering to us ward; not willing that any should perish, but that all should come to repentance."**

There is only *one* person who holds the key that can unlock the padlock shown on the front cover. He alone can cause those iron chains to break and collapse to the ground once and for all. He is God's only Son, who came from Heaven to become man, so that He could take on the sin penalty of mankind. His name is the **"Name above all names** (Philippians 2: 9-11)," Jesus Christ! Do you know Him?

Chapter Two

WILL THE REAL JESUS PLEASE STAND UP?

The Bible tells the factual story of the creation of man, the Fall of Man into sin and the redemption plan of God through Jesus Christ. Many of the religions that we will investigate acknowledge the man known as Jesus, but their understanding of who He is and what He came to accomplish by His birth, death and resurrection are all wrong.

The Word of God warns us concerning **"another Jesus"** and **"another gospel"** in 2 Corinthians 11: 3-4, where it states, **"But I fear, lest by any means, as the serpent beguiled Eve through his subtlety, so your minds should be corrupted from the simplicity that is in Christ. For if he who comes preaching another Jesus, whom we have not preached, or if you receive another spirit which you have not received, or another gospel, which you have not accepted, you might well bear with him."** If this Scripture is carefully read, it is evident that **"another Jesus"** and **"another gospel"** are fabrications of the serpent of Genesis, Satan.

There are countless religious books, but the Bible is the only book that is inspired by the Holy Spirit. The Apostle Paul said in 2 Timothy 3: 16 that **"All Scripture is given by inspiration of God, and is profitable for doctrine, for reproof, for correction, for instruction in righteousness."** Because of this fact, the answers given in this book will be taken from the

Bible, which I personally trust to be the gold standard for absolute truth.

In order to create a baseline for comparison to all of the other religions we will eventually cover, it seems fitting to establish exactly who the Bible says Jesus truly is and why He came to Earth in the first place. In John 1: 1 and 14, it is revealed that, **"In the beginning was the Word, and the Word was *with* God, and the Word *was* God... And the Word was made flesh, and dwelt among us** (My italics)."

These verses are referring to Jesus, who is the living Word of God and who was created before the foundation of the world (1 Peter 1: 20). The Old Testament Scriptures point forward to the coming of Jesus Christ, while the New Testament Scriptures point back to what Jesus did when He died on the Cross to save those who would believe in His once and for all sacrifice. These verses also proclaim the deity of Jesus Christ and go on to explain that He was incarnated as a man and dwelt here on Earth for a time.

A few verses later in John 1: 29, John the Baptist sees Jesus walking toward him and says, **"...Behold the Lamb of God, which takes away the sin of the world."** The reason that Jesus came from Heaven to Earth was to take away the sin of mankind. But how did humanity get into this predicament in the first place?

When God created Adam and Eve, He had fashioned a perfect world with no sin, sickness or death. Adam and Eve were given free will to choose whether or not they would obey God. He had planned for mankind to live on forever in their human bodies, but something happened that ruined God's perfect design. Romans 6: 23 aptly states, **"For the wages of sin is death..."**

In regard to Adam and Eve, it says in Genesis 2: 16-17, **"And the LORD God commanded the man, saying, Of every tree of the Garden you may freely eat: But of the tree of the knowledge of good and evil, you shall not eat of it for in the day that you eat thereof you shall surely die."** Most of us are acquainted with the story of the Fall of Man, when Satan spoke through a serpent and coerced Eve into taking of the forbidden fruit. She then gave the fruit to Adam, causing man to fall from God's grace.

Because every natural human comes from Adam, the sin nature was passed on to each and every person born after him. Romans 5: 12 says, **"Wherefore, as by one man sin entered into the world, and death by sin; and so death passed upon all men, for that all have sinned."** This was the predicament that Adam and Eve caused by their disobedience to God's command. Was it possible for man to get back into a proper relationship with God?

After Adam and Eve took of the forbidden fruit, it states in Genesis 3: 7, **"And the eyes of them both were opened, and they knew that they were naked; and they sewed fig leaves together, and made themselves aprons."** When Adam and Eve's eyes were opened, they became ashamed of their nakedness and sewed fig leaves together as an apron to cover their sinfulness. This covering was made with their own hands and would have eventually withered and need to be replaced with new fig leaves.

God intervened and it says in Genesis 3: 21, **"Unto Adam also and his wife did the LORD God make coats of skins, and clothed them."** God was showing Adam and Eve that the works of their own hands were not adequate to cover their shameful sin. But, most importantly, the blood shed by the animal for Adam and Eve's covering was to represent the blood that Jesus would shed on the Cross for the sins of humanity some 4,000 years later.

God then promises a Redeemer through the seed of the woman, whom Satan had used to destroy the human race. God speaks to the serpent in Genesis 3: 15, saying, **"And I will put enmity between you and the woman, and between your seed and her Seed** (Jesus); **it shall bruise your head** (the victory that Jesus won at the Cross), **and you shall bruise His heel** (the sufferings of Jesus at the Cross).**⁴** This Scripture reveals that the woman would bring forth a Redeemer, who would bruise the head of the serpent and destroy him.

From that point forward, mankind was to look forward to the coming Redeemer. God required a substitute sacrifice for sin from the time of Adam until the time that Jesus paid the final price for sin on the Cross. We will talk more about the substitute animal sacrifice and what it represented in another chapter, but it needs to be established that the sacrificial system was instituted immediately after the Fall of Man and the purpose was for the forgiveness of sin.

Because every person born after the time of Adam was born into sin, with an ensuing sin nature, no mortal man had the ability to save himself from the wages of sin. As already stated, the consequence for sin was death and an eternal separation from God the Father. A "wage" is something that must be paid; but no amount of work or even monetary payment could take care of this sin debt. It had to be paid by someone who had no sin on their record.

This is the reason that Jesus was conceived of the Holy Spirit and born of a virgin. It was because He could not be born with the stain of sin. Even Mary, the willing handmaid of God, had the tainted blood of Adam flowing through her veins. But, when the Holy Spirit visited her, as recorded in the Luke 1: 35, He placed the embryo into her womb. It is a scientific fact that the blood of a mother and a baby do not mingle while the baby grows in vitro.

God created *only* two humans without using mankind's

---

⁴ My notes in parentheses

ability to procreate. The first one was Adam, who is referred to as the **"first Man;"** and the second was the incarnated Jesus, who is called the **"second man"** or the **"last Adam"** (1 Corinthians 15: 45, 47). Jesus was born without the sin nature and He remained without sin for the entirety of His earthly life. 2 Corinthians 5: 21 states, **"For He** (God) **has made Him** (Jesus) **to be sin** (a sin-offering) **for us, Who knew no sin; that we might be made the righteousness of God in Him."** If Jesus had sinned even one time, then when He died on the Cross, He would not have been raised from the dead because, as stated, **"the wages of sin is death** (Romans 6: 23).**"**

The incarnation is recorded in Luke 1: 35, where it says, **"And the Angel answered and said unto her, The Holy Spirit shall come upon you, and the power of the Highest shall overshadow you: therefore also that the holy thing which shall be born of you shall be called the Son of God."** Another very important fact about Jesus is that He was the **"Son of God."** The famous Scripture in John 3: 16 not only proclaims this fact, but also reiterates His grand purpose. The verse says, **"For God so loved the world; that He gave His only Begotten Son, that whosoever believes in Him should not perish, but have everlasting life."**

The Bible also refers to Jesus as **"Emmanuel,"** which means "God with us." This speaks of His incarnation when He came to dwell with mortal man. Jesus walked the Earth for thirty-three and a half years and despite the fact that He was tempted, He remained without sin, which qualified Him to take our place on the Cross. Hebrews 4: 15 states, **"...but was in all points tempted like as we are, yet without sin."** We deserved the penalty of sin, but Jesus took that punishment upon Himself so that we could have eternal life in Heaven.

While we are looking at the attributes of Jesus revealed to us in the Bible, it must be said that He is the one and only mediator between man and God. We cannot reach God without going through Jesus Christ. 1 Timothy 2: 5-6 says, **"For there is one God, and one Mediator between God and men, the Man Christ Jesus; who gave Himself a ransom for all, to be testified in due time."**

Did you know that there are over 300 prophecies in the Bible concerning Jesus Christ? God devoted approximately one third of the Bible to prophecy and one fourth of the Bible to predictive prophecy.[5] Prophecy is best defined as *history written in advance.* In 2 Peter 1: 21, it states, **"For the Prophecy came not in the old time by the will of man: but Holy men of God spoke as they were moved by the Holy Spirit."** God, the Holy Spirit, gave these prophets the words to speak and oftentimes, they were not well-received.

The purpose of these prophecies was to prepare God's chosen people for the coming Redeemer, which He had promised to send them in Genesis 3: 15. Jesus fulfilled every single prophecy concerning His first coming and, no doubt, He will fulfill the prophecies of His imminent second coming. Acts 3: 18 says, **"But those things, which God before had showed by the mouth of all His Prophets, that Christ should suffer, He has so fulfilled."** The fulfillment of every single one of these prophecies should give credibility to the Bible, the source of absolute truth.

True prophets of God will have a 100% accuracy rate. There are three principles by which all true prophecy should be tested[6]:

---

[5] *All the Messianic Prophecies of the Bible*, Herbert Lockyer, Zondervan Publishing, Grand Rapids, Michigan, 1973, page 10

[6] *All the Messianic Prophecies of the Bible*, Herbert Lockyer, Zondervan Publishing, Grand Rapids, Michigan, 1973, page 21

- It must be such an unveiling of the future that no mere human foresight or wisdom could have guessed it.
- The prediction must deal in sufficient details to exclude shrewd guesswork.
- There must be such a lapse of time between the prophecy and the fulfillment as precludes the agency of the prophet himself in effecting or affecting the result.

Judging by the standards listed above, all of the Messianic prophecies prove to be legitimate. Joshua 21: 45 states, **"There failed not ought of any good thing which the Lord has spoken to the house of Israel; all came to pass."** Most of the prophecies were given 800 to 1,000 years before their actual fulfillment. Here are some examples of the hundreds of prophecies proclaimed in the Bible concerning Jesus:

- The virgin birth was prophesied in Isaiah 7: 14 where it says, **"Therefore the Lord Himself shall give you a sign; Behold, a virgin shall conceive, and bear a son, and shall call His name Immanuel."** This was spoken in 742 B.C. which means that this prophecy came to pass 742 years later as the account given in Luke 1: 31-33, when the angel Gabriel appears to Mary and says, **"And, behold, you shall conceive in your womb, and bring forth a Son, and shall call His name JESUS. He shall be great, and shall be called the Son of the Highest: and the Lord God shall give unto Him the throne of His father David: And He shall reign over the house of**

Jacob forever; and of His Kingdom there shall be no end."

- In Micah 5: 2, it says, "**But you, Bethlehem... out of you shall He come forth unto Me who is to be Ruler of Israel...**" This prediction came to pass in Matthew 2: 4, where it states, "**Now when Jesus was born in Bethlehem of Judea...**" There is also an account in John 7: 42 that proclaims Bethlehem as the birthplace of Jesus.

- Zechariah 11: 12 states, "**...So they weighed for My price thirty pieces of silver.**" The fulfillment was documented in Matthew 26: 15, where it says, "**...And they covenanted with him** (Judas) **for thirty pieces of silver.**" This was the price of a slave in that day. Judas sold Jesus out for thirty pieces of silver, which was predicted over 500 years before the actual event took place.

- Isaiah 53: 7 says, "**He was oppressed, and He was afflicted, yet He opened not His mouth: He is brought as a lamb to the slaughter, and as a sheep before her shearers is dumb, so He opens not His mouth.**" This is referring to the time when Pontius Pilate was questioning Jesus about the false accusations that the Jews had brought against Him. The fulfillment is in Matthew 27: 12-14, where it says, "**And when He was accused of the Chief Priests and Elders, He answered nothing. Then said Pilate unto Him, Do you not hear how many things they witness against you? And He answered him to never a word; insomuch that the governor marveled greatly.**" Even though Jesus was innocent of the charges, He still remained silent, just as the prophetic prediction given nearly 800 years earlier.

- Psalms 109: 4 and Isaiah 53: 12 both state, "**... and He bore the sins of many, and made intercession for the transgressors.**" The fulfillment of this prophecy is found in Luke 23: 34, where it says, "**Then said Jesus, Father, forgive them for they know not what they do.**"

- Isaiah 53: 9, 12, **"And He made His grave with the wicked and with the rich in His death; because He had done no violence, neither was any deceit in His mouth...He was numbered with the transgressors."** This prophecy was fulfilled in two different ways. First of all, the fulfillment was recorded in Mark 15: 27 where it says, **"And with Him they crucify two thieves; the one on His right hand, and the other on His left."** Here, Jesus made His grave with the wicked; but the prophecy says **"He made his grave with the wicked *and* with the rich in His death** (My italics)." Jesus made His grave with the rich when Joseph of Arimathaea, a wealthy man, was kind enough to help prepare the body of Jesus after His death, as well as, donate his own tomb for Jesus' body to be laid to rest. This account is given in Matthew 27: 57-60 where it says, **"When the evening was come, there came a rich man of Arimathaea, named Joseph, who also himself was Jesus' disciple: He went to Pilate, and begged the body of Jesus. Then Pilate commanded the body to be delivered. And when Joseph had taken the body, he wrapped it in a clean linen cloth, and laid it in his own new tomb..."**
- Psalms 22: 18 says, **"They part my garments among them, and cast lots upon my vesture."** Then in John 19: 23, 24, this prophecy came to pass when it states, **"Then the soldiers, when they had crucified Jesus, took His garments...They said therefore among themselves, Let us not rend it, but cast lots for it, whose it shall be."** There are 1,000 years between the prophecy and the fulfillment here!
- In Psalms 34: 20, David said, **"He keeps all his bones: not one of them is broken."** This prophecy and custom came to reality shortly after the death of Jesus, as documented in John 19: 31-33 where it says, **"The Jews, therefore, because it was the preparation** (of the Passover meal), **that the bodies**

should not remain upon the Cross on the Sabbath Day, (for that Sabbath Day was a high day,) besought Pilate that their legs might be broken, and that they might be taken away. Then came the soldiers, and broke the legs of the first, and of the other which was crucified with Him. But when they came to Jesus, and saw that He was dead already, they broke not His legs..."

The Jesus of the Bible has many names which describe Him perfectly. Here are some of them with the Scripture addresses included:

- Almighty One (Revelation 1: 8)
- Alpha and Omega (Revelation 22: 13)
- Advocate (1 John 2: 1)
- Author and Perfecter of our Faith (Hebrews 12: 2)
- Bread of Life (John 6: 35)
- Beloved Son of God (Matthew 3: 17)
- Bridegroom (Matthew 9: 15)
- Chief Cornerstone (Psalm 118: 22)
- Deliverer (1 Thessalonians 1: 10)
- Faithful and True (Revelation 19: 11)
- Good Shepherd (John 10: 11)
- Great High Priest (Hebrews 4: 14)
- Head of the Church (Ephesians 1: 22)
- Holy Servant (Acts 4: 29-30)
- I Am (John 8: 58)
- Emmanuel (Isaiah 7: 14)
- Indescribable Gift (2 Corinthians 9: 15)
- Judge (Acts 10: 42)
- King of Kings and Lord of Lords (Revelation 17: 4)
- Lamb of God (John 1: 29)
- Light of the World (John 8: 12)

- Lion of the Tribe of Judah (Revelation 5: 5)
- Lord of All (Philippians 2: 9-11)
- Mediator (1 Timothy 2: 5)
- Messiah (John 1: 41)
- Mighty One (Isaiah 60: 16)
- One Who Sets Free (John 8: 36)
- Our Hope (1 Timothy 1: 1)
- Our Peace (Ephesians 2: 14)
- Redeemer (Job 19: 25)
- Risen Lord (1 Corinthians 15: 3-4)
- Rock (1 Corinthians 10: 4)
- Sacrifice for Our Sins (1 John 4: 10)
- Saviour (Luke 2: 11)
- Son of Man (Luke 19: 10)
- Son of the Most High (Luke 1: 32)
- Supreme Creator (1 Corinthians 1: 16-17)
- Resurrection and the Life (John 11: 25)
- The Door (John 10: 9)
- The Way (John 14: 6)
- The Word (John 1: 1)
- True Vine (John 15: 1)
- Truth (John 8: 32)
- Victorious One (Revelation 3: 21)
- Wonderful (Isaiah 9: 6)
- Counselor (Isaiah 9: 6)
- Mighty God (Isaiah 9: 6)
- Everlasting Father (Isaiah 9: 6)
- Prince of Peace (Isaiah 9: 6)

The Bible repeatedly gives a clear picture of Jesus and His great significance. As already mentioned, Jesus Christ is the **"Name above all names** (Philippians 2: 9-11)." No other person mentioned in the Bible is described in such detail, because the story of the Bible is **"Jesus Christ and Him Crucified** (1 Corinthians 2: 2)."

Other religions that acknowledge Jesus, view Him as a good man, an example, a leader, a healer, a miracle man, and sometimes even a prophet. Jesus was all of these, but they do not recognize the most important attribute, which was that *He is the Son of God who died on the Cross to take away the sin of the world.* Simple faith in this fact is what redeems a person.

The word "Gospel" means "good news." The true Gospel, as given to us in the Bible, is that despite the fact that man was born with the sin nature, there is a second chance for redemption through the blood of Jesus Christ. Isaiah 1: 18 says, **"Come now, and let us reason together saith the LORD: though your sins be as scarlet, they shall be as white as snow; though they be red like crimson, they shall be as wool."** I would say that is certainly good news!

You are saved when you admit that you were born a sinner and accept that Jesus was the Son of God who died on the Cross to pay your sin debt. That is the pure and simple Gospel! God makes it easy enough for even a young child to comprehend because, as I already stated, He is not willing that anyone perish, but that all would to come to repentance (2 Peter 3: 9).

Religion takes God's simple plan of salvation and requires its followers to work diligently to earn redemption by good deeds, church attendance, mantras, self-deprivation, self-mutilation, praying repetitive prayers, receiving sacraments, cleansing themselves in a specific body of water, and I could go on. Religion complicates the **"simplicity that is in Christ"** and creates **"another Jesus"** and **"another gospel."** God warns us in 2 Corinthians 11: 3-4 that Satan is the author of these false ways and acceptance of **"another Jesus"** and **"another gospel"** will corrupt your mind and, therefore, your eternal soul.

Chapter Three

HOW CAN GOOD BE BAD?

God is omnipotent, omniscient and omnipresent, meaning that He is all powerful, He is all-knowing and He is everywhere, all of the time. God knows the past, the present and the future. Understanding this attribute of God, one might ask the question: *Why would God put the tree of the knowledge of good and evil in the Garden of Eden if He knew that Adam and Eve would disobey Him?* Isaiah 55: 8 says, **"For my thoughts are not your thoughts; neither are your ways my ways says the Lord."**

We have already established that God had created a perfect world for Adam and Eve. There were many trees in the Garden of Eden and plenty for them to eat without ever having to eat of the tree that God had forbidden. God's provision for Adam and Eve lacked absolutely nothing. Genesis 2: 9 states, **"And out of the ground made the LORD God to grow every tree that is pleasant to the sight, and good for food; the tree of life in the midst of the Garden..."**

I believe that the tree of the knowledge of good and evil was to provide Adam and Eve with a choice and a test of obedience. They would have only been slaves to God if He had not created them with free will. Slavery was never what God intended for His children. Because Adam and Eve were created as free moral agents, they had to be tested and the tree of the knowledge of good and evil provided such a trial.

The tree, in and of itself, was not infused with sin or evil. The fruit that grew on the tree was not poisonous, nor did it contain the magical ability to impart the knowledge of good and evil. But, eating the fruit was an act of rebellion and caused sin and death to enter God's pristine world. The ramifications of Adam's sin are so profound that they changed the entire animal kingdom, plant kingdom and most notably, the human race.

For one, the act of sin caused spiritual death because man was separated from God. But, it also brought about physical death because the tree of life was to be used for the eternal health of man. Because of Adam's disobedience, God banished Adam and Eve from the Garden of Eden and they could no longer eat from the tree of life. Genesis 3: 22, 24 explains: **"And the LORD God said, Behold, the man is become as one of Us, to know good and evil... So He drove out the man; and He placed at the east of the Garden of Eden Cherubims, and a flaming sword which turned every way, to the keep the way of the tree of life."**

Had only Eve sinned, the consequences would have been confined to her. But, because the seed of procreation lies in the man, Adam partaking of the fruit caused any human born after his time, with the exception of Jesus Christ, to be infected with the sin nature. Eve may have been deceived by Satan, but Adam *willfully disobeyed* God's command. The Apostle Paul says in 1 Timothy 2: 14, **"And Adam was not deceived, but the woman being deceived was in the transgression."** God knew that Adam would fail and that is why He provided the cure for the sin problem.

Jesus took away sin, along with the power of sin, when He died on the Cross in our place. But, He also defeated Satan, who brought sin and death into this world at the Fall of Man. Colossians 2: 14-15 states, **"Blotting out the handwriting of Ordinances that was against us, which was contrary to us, and took it out of the way, nailing it to His Cross; And having spoiled principalities and powers, He made a show of them openly, triumphing over them in it."** The **"principalities and powers"** mentioned above represent Satan and his fallen angels. Because Jesus was triumphant over the powers of darkness, we too can have victory if we accept that His death on the Cross saves us.

So, what is meant by "good" and "evil" when the Bible speaks of the tree of the knowledge of good and evil? Before their disobedience, Adam and Eve were oblivious concerning evil. They were originally created to be in complete harmony with God and knew only goodness and righteousness. Unfortunately, curiosity destroyed their relationship with God and caused a separation from Him, which man could not restore on his own accord. God is always good; it is the rejection of God that is the embodiment of evil. Where did this evil originate?

Sometime in eternity past, the archangel Lucifer led a rebellion in Heaven and when God cast him out, one third of the angels followed. The Bible reveals only a fragment of information concerning Lucifer's revolt and his motives. Isaiah 14: 11-14 states, **"Your pomp is brought down to the grave, and the noise of your viols, the worm is spread under you, and the worms cover you. How art thou fallen from Heaven, O Lucifer, son of the morning! How art thou cut down to the ground, which did weaken the nations! For you have said in your heart, I will ascend into Heaven, I will exalt my throne above the stars of God: I will sit also upon the mount of the congregation, in the sides of the north: I will ascend above the heights of the clouds; I will be like the Most High."**

Lucifer originally held a high position among the angels in Heaven, until iniquity was found in him. Ezekiel 28: 12 describes Lucifer when it states, **"...You seal up the sum, full of wisdom, and perfect beauty."** But it seems that his wisdom and beauty were the very reasons that Lucifer revolted in the first place. Ezekiel 28: 15, 17 reveals, **"You were perfect in your ways from the day that you were created, till iniquity was found in you... Your heart was lifted up because of your beauty, you have corrupted your wisdom by reason of your brightness..."**

In Hebrew, the name "Lucifer" means "the bright and shining one" or "light bearer." These attributes and his exalted position caused Lucifer to be vain and full of pride. As a result, he sought to exalt his own throne above God's by leading a revolution. Lucifer used his great wisdom to deceive the angels under his dominion into following him into rebellion against God. With Lucifer's revolution, the spirit world was divided into the two opposing forces of good and evil.

Lucifer became known by many names, one of them being "Satan." In Genesis Chapter 3: 1, we are introduced to Satan where the Bible says, **"Now the serpent was more subtle than any beast of the field, which the LORD God had made."** Initially, God had created mankind in His likeness to be His companions and before the Fall, He would walk with Adam and Eve in the Garden of Eden. God took great joy in all of His creation. It was Satan who spoke to Eve through the serpent in the Garden of Eden.

Genesis 3: 1 goes on to state, **"And he said unto the woman, Yes, has God said, You shall not eat of every tree of the Garden?"** Eve tells Satan how God had commanded them that they could eat of any tree except of **"the tree of the knowledge of good and evil,"** because they would die if they partook of the fruit of that tree. The serpent responds in Genesis 3: 4 by saying, **"You shall not surely die..."** He cunningly puts doubt in Eve's mind about God's warning and then proceeds to tell her in Genesis 3: 5, **"For God does know that in the day you eat thereof , then your eyes shall be opened, and you shall be as gods, knowing good and evil."**

Understanding the "evil" side of the tree of knowledge is not that difficult to comprehend, but it is the knowledge of "good" that puzzles most people. What is meant by the words "the knowledge of good"? It refers to the "good" that man does in an attempt to earn himself favor or eternal salvation from God. This type of "good" covers a broad spectrum of works. Because socially, good works are seen as admirable to most people looking in from the outside, it is hard to argue that they are not *good* in the eyes of God *if they are being used to earn something from Him.*

Now, on the contrary, when someone has been born again of the Spirit, and transformed into serving God out of complete love and devotion, then that person will perform works for the Kingdom of God. The difference is that he is not doing good to tip the scale in God's favor, but only in love and appreciation for God.

I will give a short personal testimony of my experience because I feel it might relate to others who have made the same mistake. Before I was saved in 2005, I was under the impression that salvation was based on a scale of good deeds versus evil deeds. As a member of a prominent religion for the first thirty-two years of my life, I didn't know any other way. I felt as if I was on the hamster wheel of life, always trying to make sure that the scale was tipping in the right direction of God's favor.

I often worried if the good deeds were enough to save me and I certainly did not have any assurance of my soul's eternal salvation. When my eyes were opened to the truth of the Gospel of Jesus Christ and I accepted His sacrifice on my behalf, I felt a heavy weight lift from my body, like the chains that had bound me for thirty-two years had finally come crashing down. Instantly, I was seeing through clearer eyes and I knew I had been saved from the fires of Hell. It truly was a miraculous day because God had been dealing with me for quite a while to give my life to Him. He graciously put me in the position where I would have the opportunity to either accept or reject His beckoning call.

Then, as a newly saved person, I tried desperately to please God and live a holy life. I finally felt assured of my salvation, but living a life that was pleasing to God was not so easy. I was trying to get victory over things that I knew did not please God, but I was trying to break those bondages in my own strength. The end result was failure and it was a very discouraging time in my walk with the Lord.

I felt that everyone who knew me was now watching me closely because I had made the proclamation that now I was a "born again Christian." But, I was trying by the works of my own flesh to get victory and please God by reading my Bible, praying, going to church, etc. While these works did help me to grow in the Lord, *my motives were all wrong*. God quickly convicted me and showed me that I should never do those things to gain his favor, but because I love Him and because I want to learn more about Him. What I came to learn is that the only thing that is pleasing to God is our faith in the finished work of Jesus on the Cross.

When we place our faith in Jesus' once and for all sacrifice, then the Holy Spirit will work on our behalf to show us how to live victoriously for God. How? Well, for one we will feel conviction if we are headed in the wrong direction or if we are taking part in sin. God is always there to forgive us and change our desires if we will yield and let Him. Also, the Holy Spirit will gently nudge us as God opens doors for job opportunities, relationships, everyday living and the chance to share the Gospel with others. But at the same time, the Holy Spirit will give us peace when God closes doors that might be detrimental to our walk with Him.

Jesus speaks of the Holy Spirit in John 14: 16 and 26 saying, **"And I will pray the Father, and He shall give you another Comforter, that He may abide with you forever... But the Comforter, which is the Holy Spirit, whom the Father will send in My name, He shall teach you all things, and bring all things to your remembrance, whatsoever I have said unto you."** And in Luke 24: 49 Jesus says, **"And, behold, I send the Promise of My Father upon you: but tarry ye in the city of Jerusalem, until you be endued with power from on high."**

After Jesus' ascension into Heaven, the **"Promise of My**

Father," that would be poured out on His disciples was the mighty Baptism in the Holy Spirit. This is recorded in Acts 2: 1-4 where it states, **"And when the Day of Pentecost was fully come, they were all with one accord in one place. And suddenly there came a sound from Heaven as of a rushing mighty wind, and it filled all the house where they were sitting, And there appeared unto them cloven tongues like as of fire, and it sat upon each of them. And they were all filled with the Holy Spirit, and began to speak with other tongues, as the Spirit gave them utterance."**

When Jesus told His disciples that He had to go away, they were, no doubt, emotionally distraught. They looked to Him as their teacher and sought continual advice about where to go and what to do. Jesus tells them that they will not be abandoned, but that God will send them **"a Comforter,"** who will teach them all things. The same is true for any believer today. The Holy Spirit is available any time of day to comfort, teach and help us to live a holy Christian. It simply takes us denying our own abilities and letting the Holy Spirit guide and lead us every second of the day.

Romans 8: 11 states, **"But if the Spirit of Him who raised Jesus from the dead dwell in you, He who raised up Christ from the dead shall also quicken your mortal bodies by His Spirit that dwells in you."** By saying "yes" to Jesus' finished work on the Cross, it gives the Holy Spirit the freedom to strengthen us to overcome sin, as well as, Satan's vicious assaults. We can truly have peace in the midst of the storm when we understand that God is in control and that He has provided us with everything we need.

This formula helps tremendously to understand how to live a victorious Christian life by denying self and looking to the Lord God for every need:

- FOCUS: *Jesus Christ*, the Son of God who died for the sins of mankind.
- OBJECT OF FAITH: *The finished work of Jesus on the Cross*, which gives the Holy Spirit the liberty to help us when we deny our own self efforts.
- POWER SOURCE: *The Holy Spirit*. As a believer, we must be sensitive to the Holy Spirit's conviction and direction.
- RESULTS: *Victory* over the world, the flesh and the Devil!

Now, the following is what occurs when an unbeliever, and even a believer, uses a different formulation in an attempt to gain victory:

- FOCUS: *Good works* to earn something from God.
- OBJECT OF FAITH: Focusing on works, the object of faith becomes their own *performance*.
- POWER SOURCE: When we are focused on works and our own performance, then the power source becomes our *own self, abilities and strength*. The Holy Spirit cannot help us when we operate in the flesh.
- RESULTS: *Failure* is the result. Even if there is victory for a time, it will eventually end in defeat if this formula is used.

The reason for the failure is explained by the Apostle Paul in 1 Corinthians 1: 18, where He says, **"For the preaching of the Cross is to them that perish foolishness; but unto us which are saved, it is the power of God."** Those who want to discount the great victory that Jesus won on the Cross for us, believe that placing their faith in His finished work is **"foolishness."** But Paul clearly states that these people will **"perish,"** which means an eternity in the Lake of Fire. On the contrary, He states that those who hear the **"preaching of the Cross"** and accept it, are not only saved, but that it is **"the power of God."**

A few verses later, recorded in 1 Corinthians 1: 23, Paul says, **"But we preach Christ Crucified, unto the Jews a stumbling block, and unto the Greeks, foolishness."** Paul, the Apostle to the Gentiles, preached **"Jesus Christ and Him Crucified** (1 Corinthians 2: 2)"** for salvation and also for sanctification. Sanctification is to be set apart for the work of God. But, we must understand that every single man-made religion denies the finished work of Jesus on the Cross and instead, requires their faithful to earn salvation by good works and self-effort.

What these religions are essentially stating, whether they realize it or not, is that Jesus' death on the Cross was not sufficient to redeem mankind. They feel the need to add to Jesus' sacrifice by works of the flesh. The famous Scripture in Ephesians 2: 8-9 sets the record straight when it states, **"For by grace you are saved through faith; and that not of yourselves: it is the Gift of God not of works, lest any man should boast."** Jesus' sacrifice was a free gift from God and no one can argue that paying back the gift-giver would be disrespectful. That is exactly how God feels when we attempt to add to what Jesus accomplished on the Cross for us with our own good works.

Please be mindful of your motives when it pertains to good deeds and service to the Lord. As we have already stated, the good works will follow those who are born again of the Spirit and sold out to God's will in their lives. But the "good" of the tree of the knowledge of good and evil can also be a hindrance to our eternal soul if we are using the deeds to gain something from God outside of faith in Jesus' once and for all sacrifice.

Here is portion of a devotional reading from *My Utmost for His Highest* by Oswald Chambers:

> The call of God is not a call to serve Him in any particular way. My contact with the nature of God will shape my understanding of His call and will help me

33

realize what I truly desire to do for Him....

Service is the overflow which pours from a life filled with love and devotion. But strictly speaking, there is no *call* to that. Service is what I bring to the relationship and is the reflection of my identification with the nature of God. Service becomes a natural part of my life. God brings me into proper relationship with Himself so that I can understand His call, and then I serve Him on my own out of motivation of absolute love. Service to God is the deliberate love-gift of a nature that has heard the call of God. Service is an expression of my nature, and God's call is an expression of His nature. Therefore, when I receive His nature and hear His call, His divine voice resounds throughout His nature and mine and the two become one in service. The Son of God reveals Himself in me, and out of devotion to Him, service becomes my everyday way of life.[7]

So, what kind of knowledge does God truly want to impart to His creation? 2 Corinthians 4: 6 sums it up quite well when Paul states, **"For God, who commanded the light to shine out of darkness, has shined in our hearts, to give the light of the knowledge of the glory of God in the face of Jesus Christ."**

---

[7] *My Utmost for His Highest,* Oswald Chambers, 1935 Original publication, revised in 1992, Discovery House Publishers, January 17th devotion

Chapter Four

THE TWO ALTARS

When we come to understand God's plan of salvation in providing a substitute sacrifice following the Fall of Man, there is great significance in the story of Cain and Abel. God reveals to us the two prospective routes that man can choose when attempting to please Him. One way is praised and accepted by God; while the other way is rejected and cursed. We should pay very close attention to the account of Cain and Abel, because it impacts each person's eternal standing with God.

In the last chapter, the story of Adam and Eve and the Fall of Man was explained. Any person born of the seed of Adam would inherit the curse of the sin nature. Unfortunately, because Adam sinned, He and Eve would experience great heartache when their own flesh and blood would commit an unthinkable act.

In Genesis 4: 1, it states, **"And Adam knew Eve his wife and she conceived and bear Cain, and said, I have gotten a man from the Lord."** If you will remember, in Genesis 3: 15, God promised to send Adam and Eve a Redeemer. So, by Eve using the term **"Lord,"** which means, "Covenant God," she was under the impression that Cain was the Promised One.

Unfortunately, Eve did not realize that nothing good could come from sinful flesh. The Redeemer would not be conceived by mankind, but by the Holy Spirit. He would have to born without human procreation to be void of the sin nature. Remember, Jesus Christ was conceived of the Holy Spirit and born of a virgin, therefore, born without the curse of the Fall of Man.

Look at the contrast given in Romans Chapter 5 comparing Adam, the **"first man,"** with Jesus, who is the **"last Adam"** and the **"second man** (1 Corinthians 15: 45, 47).**"** Paul states in Romans 5: 15-19:[8]

- **"For if through the offence of one** (Adam) **many be dead, much more the Grace of God, and the Gift by Grace, which is by one Man, Jesus Christ, has abounded unto many."**
- **"And not as it was by one** (Adam) **who sinned, so is the gift** (Jesus): **for the judgment was by one** (Adam) **to condemnation, but the Free Gift** (Jesus) **is of many offences unto Justification."**
- **"For if by one man's offence death reigned by one** (Adam)**; much more they which receive abundance of Grace and the Gift of Righteousness shall reign in life by One, Jesus Christ."**
- **"Therefore as by the offence of one** (Adam) **judgment came upon all men to condemnation; even so by the Righteousness of One** (Jesus) **the Free Gift came upon all men unto Justification of life."**
- **"For as by one man's** (Adam) **disobedience many were made sinners, so by the obedience of One** (Jesus) **shall many be made Righteous."**

The descriptions given above concerning Jesus could never be said of any person born from the seed of Adam. By the time Adam and Eve's second son, Abel, was born, Eve had come to the realization that Cain was not the Promised Seed. The name

---

[8] My notes in parentheses

Abel means, "vanity," and shows that Eve had lost hope of her conceiving the Redeemer. Cain and Abel were born outside of Paradise because they were the sons of fallen Adam, who by his disobedience brought sin and death into the world, just as the previous Scriptures repeatedly confirm.

The Bible indicates that both Cain and Abel had honorable professions. Genesis 4: 2 says, **"...And Abel was a keeper of the sheep, but Cain was a tiller of the ground."** Some may claim that their occupations had an impact on what they would give back to God as sacrifices, but we must understand that the sacrificial system had been explained to Adam and Eve and the knowledge was most certainly passed onto their offspring.

Let's reiterate exactly what the sacrifice was to be and what it represented. From the moment of the Fall of Man, God made it clear that an innocent animal was to be used as a sacrifice for sin. The animal was meant to be a substitute, which represented the coming Redeemer. They were, by faith, to look forward to the Promised Seed, and in the meantime, display their faith by offering up an innocent animal for worship and especially for any transgression against God. The animal was meant to cover the sin, which kept them in a state of righteousness. This was the *only way* to stay in God's good graces, until the Redeemer would come.

No doubt, Cain and Abel were both brought up knowing to bring an animal sacrifice to the altar. *In the Bible, the altar always represents the Cross.* Genesis 4: 3 records, **"And in the process of time it came to pass, that Cain brought of the fruit of the ground an offering unto the Lord."** This offering was the fruit of his hands, and despite how beautiful and even how delicious the fruit of the ground might have been, it was not what God had required. Likely, Cain worked hard to produce the offering, yet what was God's reaction?

Genesis 4: 5 states, **"But unto Cain and his offering He had not respect..."** Because it was the innocent animal that represented the coming Redeemer, in effect, Cain was showing that he had no need of a Saviour and could save himself with the fruits of his labor. As a result, God had no respect for Cain's offering.

God required the shedding of blood to remove the curse and to cover sin. Cain's sacrifice was an *unbloody sacrifice*, which was ineffective against sin. In the context of sin, Hebrews 9: 22 states, **"...without the shedding of blood, there is no remission."** Remember that the penalty of sin was death (Romans 6: 23), and this stood between Cain and his relationship with God. Within Cain's offering there was no death of an innocent animal and no acknowledgment of the coming Redeemer. That is why it was rejected by God.

What was Cain's reaction to God's refusal of his unbloody sacrifice? The Bible says in Genesis 4: 5, **"And Cain was very angry and his countenance fell."** Instead of repenting before the Lord, Cain was **"very angry.** *" Anger, in one form or another, is a byproduct of self-righteousness.* And if we breakdown the word "self-righteousness," it simply means trying to attain righteousness by our own self efforts, which is precisely what Cain was doing.

God even gave Cain a chance to make things right. It says in Genesis 4: 6-7, **"And the LORD said unto Cain, Why are you angry? And why is your countenance fallen? If you do well, shall you not be accepted? And if you do not well, sin lies at the door. And unto you shall his desire, and you shall rule over him."** God is telling Cain that if he makes the proper sacrifice, then it would be accepted. Also, God says that He will give Cain the birthright, meaning he would be the next in line when Adam dies. But, God also warns Cain that if he does not repent, then **"sin lies at the door."**

Cain represents the man of religion, who wants to fashion his own way to God. Unfortunately, God will not accept our works as a means to earn anything from Him. God made it clear that to appease Him, the blood of an innocent animal had to be shed. God, in His foreknowledge, knew that Jesus would one day be that sinless **"Lamb of God,"** who would go the Cross to be offered as a substitute sacrifice for the sins of mankind. That is why the proper offering was commanded.

In contrast, Cain's younger brother, Abel, also made a sacrifice to God. In Genesis 4: 4, it reads, **"And Abel he also brought of the firstlings of his flock and the fat thereof, and the LORD had respect unto Abel and his offering."** Abel brought God exactly what He desired, and God accepted it with great respect for Abel. *While Cain represents religious man, Abel characterizes a man of faith.* He is an example to every person desiring a true relationship with God. Abel was made righteous through to the blood of a blameless animal, just as we can be made righteous by placing our faith in the spotless blood of the **"Lamb of God,"** Jesus Christ.

Abel's altar represents *true repentance and faith in the blood of the coming Redeemer.* Cain's altar epitomized *pride, unbelief in God's chosen way and self-righteousness.* Abel's altar was offensive to man's eye, but to God, it was perfect. Cain's altar was beautiful to man, but revolting to God.

When God accepted Abel's sacrifice and questioned Cain concerning his willingness to repent and offer properly, it caused great anger to envelope Cain. He could not hide his anger and because he could not take out his wrath on God, Cain chose to take out the revenge on Abel. All Cain had to do was simply tell God that he was sorry and offer an innocent animal. His religion was too refined to kill a guiltless animal, but not too refined to kill his own flesh and blood brother.

Genesis 4: 8 gives this account saying, **"And Cain talked with Abel his brother: and it came to pass when they were in the field, that Cain rose up against Abel his brother and slew him."** Refusal to obey God only drives an individual deeper into sin and ultimately to self-destruction. The only way to stop the downhill spiral is by repenting and placing our faith in Jesus' finished work on the Cross. This is where Satan, the author of sin, was defeated (Colossians 2: 14-15)! Acts 20: 21 explains this by stating, **"Repentance toward God, and faith toward our Lord Jesus Christ."**

Even though Cain felt that his sacrifice was good, God made it clear that it was insufficient. As stated above, in Genesis 4: 6-7, God gave him a second chance to do what Acts 20: 21 states and repent toward God. But, as the Scripture indicates, God also required Cain to make the proper sacrifice, which would display that his faith was toward the Promised Seed. So, while repentance is good in the eyes of God, it must be followed by faith evidenced in Jesus' once and for all sacrifice.

Concerning Abel's murder, it should be of no surprise that down through the ages, religious man has done precisely what Cain did to Abel. They have persecuted and killed multiple millions of believers in Christ under the banner of religion. Much of the bloodshed of the past and of the present can be tied to religion.

I believe that it is evident from the Scriptures what pleases God. Even though Adam brought sin and death into the world and death passed onto all who would be born after him, God made sure that man would have a second chance to break the curse of sin and be redeemed. Sin is an ugly thing, and that is why an innocent animal had to be slaughtered. It was to show the terrible consequences of transgressing against God.

What pleased God in the Old Testament times from Adam until the birth of Christ was faith in the coming Redeemer. This was displayed with the animal sacrifices. But in the New Testament, after Jesus' death on the Cross, pleasing God means denying our own abilities to save ourselves by keeping our faith in what Jesus accomplished by His death on the Cross.

Cain's altar caused him to murder his own brother and to be cursed by God (Genesis 4: 8-15). This is indicative of religious man, who, in self-righteousness, produces what he sees fit to please God. Look at the results; they are not pleasant. History proves this fact. But in contrast, Abel's altar was accepted by God because it represented the coming Promised One by shedding the blood of a blameless animal. Abel looked forward to God's promise and exhibited his faith in a way that was pleasing to God. Understanding these facts, I must ask the question: *At which of the two altars will God find you?*

Chapter Five

A MUCH BETTER COVENANT

In the last chapter, the Old Testament plan of salvation compared to the New Testament plan was briefly mentioned. *The word "testament" means "covenant."* The Old and New Testaments of the Bible are referring to the Old Covenant that God made with His chosen people, as well as, the New Covenant, which includes **"whosever believes (1 John 5: 1)."**

While the Old Covenant required a sinner to slaughter an innocent animal to cover sin, the New Covenant is a much better covenant. Why? Because it only requires faith in the **"Lamb of God"** who was **"slain from the foundation of the world (Revelation 13: 8)."** Also, the blood of Jesus does not merely cover sin, but it **"takes away the sin of the world (John 1: 29)."** This will be explained in greater detail as this chapter unfolds.

God has made it so easy to accept His redemption plan, but nevertheless, the majority of mankind have rejected it and replaced it with some form of religion or have created their own pursuit to attain eternal life. God explains so many different ways in His Word that those who reject His free gift of salvation will be cast into the Lake of Fire burning with brimstone for eternity.

Let's first discuss the Old Testament sacrificial system and explain who it was meant for and what it entailed. In order to understand, we must start with Abraham. God told Abraham in Genesis 12: 2-3, **"And I will make of you a great nation, and I will bless you, and make your name great; and you shall be a blessing: And I will bless them who bless you, and curse them who curse you: and in you shall all the families of the Earth be** blessed."

In Genesis Chapter 12, God called Abram (Abraham) out of Ur of the Chaldees, from a family of idol makers and promised him that the seed of the Redeemer would come through his lineage. Genesis 15: 6 declares why Abraham was considered righteous in the eyes of God. The Scripture states, **"And he believed in the LORD; and He counted it to him for Righteousness."** Do you see the key word here? *Abraham "believed."*

What exactly did Abraham believe? His faith was in the coming Redeemer and he proved that time and time again by making the correct sacrifice to God. Many times in the Bible, it shows that Abraham built an altar and slew an innocent animal, showing that his faith was in the spotless Lamb to come. There are many lessons that we can learn from the life of Abraham. He was not perfect and made his share of mistakes, but regardless, he was repentant and his faith was in the correct object.

Abraham was the father of Isaac and Isaac was the father of Jacob, who was later renamed "Israel," and became the father of the twelve tribes of Israel. These twelve tribes became the race known as the Israelites, God's chosen people. In other books of the Bible, they were referred to as "Hebrews," as well as, "Jews." Jesus was born into the tribe of Judah, one of the twelve sons of Jacob, and this is how the religion of Judaism acquired its name.

Deuteronomy 7: 6-8 says, **"For thou art an holy people unto the LORD thy God: the LORD thy God has chosen thee to be a special people unto Himself, above all people that are upon the face of the earth. The LORD did not set His love upon you, nor choose you, because you were more in number than any people; for you were the fewest of all people."**

God made many promises to the Jewish people concerning the land of Israel, which is their God-given homeland, and also that He would send a Redeemer to save His people from their sins.

The Jews were to watch diligently for the coming Messiah and the Old Testament Scriptures painted a picture of who God would send and the timeline when He would appear. We covered that information in a previous chapter concerning the Messianic prophecies and their fulfillments.

The story of God's chosen people is truly miraculous and reveals the mighty power and unconditional love of God. Please check out my book, *Taking the Bait*, to read more concerning the Jews and the land of Israel. I would love to elaborate more, but the purpose of this particular chapter is to discuss the two covenants given by God.

As previously mentioned, God instituted the sacrificial system after the fall of Adam. But, regrettably, the descendants of Adam and Eve became so polluted with every type of depravity that God flooded the whole Earth and saved only Noah, his wife, his three sons and their wives. This family repopulated the Earth after the Great Flood. Eventually, Abraham is introduced to us and God makes a covenant with him.

The Abrahamic Covenant, found in Genesis Chapter 15, granted the Israelites a promised land in Israel. In this covenant, God specifically promises (Genesis 12: 1-3; 13: 14-18; 15: 1-21; 17: 1-22):

- To make of Abraham a great nation, to multiply his seed exceedingly and to make him a father of many nations.
- To bless Abraham and make him great.
- To make Abraham a blessing to all of the families of the Earth.
- To bless those who bless Abraham and to curse those who curse him.
- To give Abraham and his seed forever all the land of Israel. The borders of the land are recorded in Genesis 15: 18.
- To give him a sign of the covenant, which was circumcision.

Regardless of the fact that Abraham did not live to see God's promise of a Redeemer come to pass, he kept the covenant with God and because of this, Abraham is repeatedly called **"righteous"** in passages found in Romans 4: 3; Romans 4: 9; Romans 4: 13; Galatians 3: 6; and James 2: 23.

When Jacob was patriarch, the Israelites made their way to Egypt during a terrible famine. Jacob's son, Joseph, had been sold as a slave to the Egyptians by his jealous brothers, but God allowed him to become second in command to Pharaoh. Egypt became a refuge for the Israelites, but once the Pharaoh who knew Joseph died, his successor became afraid that the Israelites would revolt. He made them slaves and treated them with great disdain.

Despite their bondage to Pharaoh, the Israelites multiplied by the millions. God called Moses to free the Israelites from under Pharaoh's control and lead them into the Promised Land of Canaan, the future land of Israel. Despite the many plagues that God called down from Heaven, Pharaoh refused to release the Children of Israel. The last plague sent by God was that the first born male of every family, even the animals, would die if Pharaoh would not free them.

Exodus Chapter 12 records God instructing Moses to tell the Israelites to slay a perfect lamb, without spot or blemish, and then to apply the blood of the lamb over their door post. When the Angel of the Lord saw the blood, it would "pass over" the house and the plague would not apply to those families. This instituted the first Passover and Jesus' death on the Cross, which occurred on the exact day of the Passover, was the very last Passover ever needed because He was the final Lamb to shed His blood for our freedom!

Once the Angel of the Lord passed over Egypt and killed all of the first born males, Pharaoh finally released the Children of Israel. God used the shed blood of a spotless lamb to rescue His people from Pharaoh, just as He would later use Jesus, a perfect sinless human, to rescue us from Satan.

Once Moses led the Children of Israel out of Egypt, they made their way through the Red Sea and into the wilderness. The Holy Spirit manifested Himself as a **"cloud by day"** and **"fire by night"** to guide the Israelites (Exodus 13: 21-22). God fed millions of people every day for forty years with manna from Heaven and miraculously gave them drink from a rock (Exodus 16: 35; 17: 6). But, because of unbelief, a journey that should have taken them only forty days ended up lasting for forty long years. And every single adult man and woman who walked out of Egypt with Moses ending up dying in the wilderness before they made it to the Promised Land. Only their children lived to see that day of God's promise being fulfilled.

But during their time in the wilderness, God gave Moses the Law, which the Children of Israel were to follow. *The purpose of the Law was to define sin.* The Mosaic Law was a long list of 613 rules which were to be followed every day. If anyone disobeyed any of these laws, it was considered sin and the individual would be required to bring a sin offering to God to atone for, or cover, the transgression. The offering involved a perfect animal, without spot or blemish, which represented the sinless perfection of Jesus. Exodus 12: 5 says, **"Your lamb shall be without blemish, a male of the first year..."**

God also gave Moses the specifications for the Tabernacle of the Congregation, which is best described as a transportable temple that the Israelites would pack up and take with them whenever they moved. I will explain the configuration in a moment, but the Tabernacle was the place where God dwelt with His chosen people on the Golden Mercy Seat, which was housed inside of the Holy of Holies.

In the case of sin, the Children of Israel were instructed to take an innocent animal to the Tabernacle of the Congregation, where a priest would go through a specific ceremony to sacrifice the animal. It involved the sinner laying hands on the animal to "transfer" the sin to the innocent victim before it was killed. Once the animal's blood was shed for the person's sin, only then was it considered atoned for in the eyes of God. However, the sin was only covered because it was not able to be taken away completely.

This ceremony of sacrificing the animal, of course, represented the blood that Jesus would shed for us on the Cross to *take away* all of our sins. Many times the animal used was a spotless lamb and this is why John the Baptist said of Jesus in John 1: 29, **"Behold the Lamb of God, which takes away the sin of the world."** Jesus was the last sin offering needed to wash away sin because He did not cover the sin, like the blood of the sacrificial animal, but He took the sin away forever! Remember that the Scripture verse in 2 Corinthians 5: 21 says, **"For He** (God) **has made Him** (Jesus) **to be sin** (a sin- offering) **for us, who knew no sin that we might be made the righteousness of God in Him."**

On the following page, there is a diagram of the Tabernacle of the Congregation. The specifications given to Moses had to be carried out exactly as God had instructed because every detail of the Tabernacle foreshadowed the Redeemer to come.

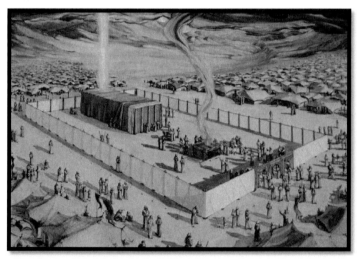

THE TABERNACLE OF THE CONGREGATION
ARIEL VIEW

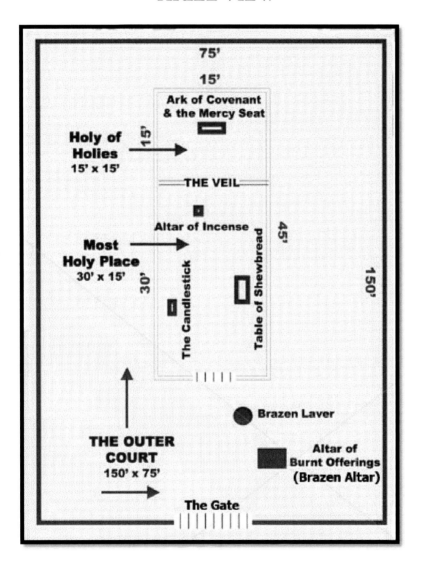

Here is an explanation of some of the details of the Tabernacle of the Congregation:

- *The Gate* was the only entrance into the Tabernacle, just as Jesus is the one and only **"gate** (Matthew 7: 13-14)**"** whereby we can have access to God the Father and to Heaven.
- *The Brazen Altar* was used to burn the animal sacrifice and the fire represented the judgment of God on the innocent victim instead of the sinner. The innocent victim, of course, represented Jesus as our sinless scapegoat.
- *The Brazen Laver* was for the washing of the priests and this speaks of the Word of God.
- *The Holy Place* housed *the Golden Lampstand* to the left, which represented Jesus as the **"Light of the World** (John 8: 12).**"**
- Also, in *the Holy Place* was *the Table of Shewbread* on the right, which held twelve cakes of bread. This bread was to remind us that Jesus is the **"Bread of Life** (John 6: 35).**"**
- *The Altar of Incense* was where the priests would take a burning coal off of *the Brazen Altar* and burn incense to God. It portrayed Jesus ever making intercession to God on our behalf (Romans 8: 34).
- *The Veil of the Temple* was a four inch thick curtain that led into *the Holy of Holies*. This veil was supernaturally torn from top to bottom the moment Jesus that died on the Cross (Matthew 27: 51; Mark 15: 38 and Luke 23: 45). This nullified the need for the animal sacrifices and also signified that we could now have access directly to God through the one and only mediator, Jesus Christ (1 Timothy 2: 5). Previously, only the High Priest could go into *the Holy of Holies* on the Day of Atonement to offer up a sacrifice for the sins of the nation of Israel, but Jesus was the very last Great High Priest ever needed (Hebrews 4: 14, 16).
- *The Holy of Holies* is where God dwelt in t*he Ark of the Covenant* from above the *Golden Mercy Seat* and between the two wings of the Cherubims (Exodus 25: 22).

The Tabernacle was a forerunner to the Jewish Temple, which was built by David's son, Solomon. That first Temple was destroyed by the Babylonian King Nebuchadnezzar and later rebuilt during the time of the Prophet Nehemiah. Then the second Temple was completely destroyed in 70 A.D. by the Roman General Titus. God allowed this because the Jewish people were still taking part in the animal sacrifices, despite the fact that Jesus Christ was the last sacrifice ever required.

The entire arrangement of the Tabernacle of the Congregation represented Jesus Christ in every single detail. The purpose of the Tabernacle and the sacrificial system was to point to the Redeemer who God would send to save His chosen people. The faith of the sinner was to be in what the sacrifice represented, not in the "religious ceremony" of it. The innocent animal paid the horrible sin penalty for the sinner, just as Jesus Christ would come and pay the sin debt for **"whosever will"** believe in His sacrifice.

51

Those who took part in the Old Testament sacrificial offerings were considered **"righteous"** by God. Unfortunately, Heaven was not accessible because of the Fall of Man. When someone under the Old Covenant died in a state of righteousness, he or she was not taken to Heaven, but to a compartment of Hell called **"Abraham's bosom"** or **"Paradise"** (Luke 16: 22, Luke 23: 43). This compartment of Hell was not the burning side of Hell where the unrighteous souls reside. Instead, it was a temporary holding spot where they were to remain until the Redeemer came to free them.

The reason why these righteous souls were not yet allowed into Heaven is because Satan still had the legal right to hold mankind captive because of the Fall of Man. The righteous dead would remain there until Jesus came and fulfilled God's plan as our Redeemer.

When Jesus died on the Cross, He went into **"Paradise,"** in the lower parts of the Earth, and released all of the righteous souls into Heaven. Let's look at Ephesians 4: 8-10 where it says, **"Wherefore He said, When He ascended up on high, He led captivity captive, and gave Gifts unto men. (Now that he ascended, what is it but that He also descended first into the lower parts of the earth? He who descended is the same also who ascended up far above all Heavens, that He might fill all things)."** Those righteous souls in Paradise, no doubt, were praying that Jesus would not change His mind because if He had not died on the Cross, then they would not have been released into Heaven, but would have remained in Paradise. Today, Paradise is completely empty!

Jesus was fully man and He was fully God. He could have taken Himself down off of the Cross, but He came to Earth for the purpose of dying to pay the penalty of sin. **"The wages of sin is death,"** (Romans 6: 23) and Jesus satisfied that debt with His own life. The rest of this Scripture reads, **"...but the Gift of God is** eternal life through Jesus Christ our Lord."

The common misconception is that Jesus was murdered. It is true that the religious Jews and the Romans mercilessly beat Jesus and put Him on the Cross, but the wounds inflicted upon Jesus did not kill Him. He died so we would not have to pay the awful sin penalty and He was the only one who could appease God because He was without sin. Isaiah 53: 5 says, **"He was wounded for *our* transgressions; he was bruised for *our* iniquities** (My italics)."** The Gospels report that Jesus **"gave up the ghost** (Mark 15: 37; Luke 23: 46 and John 19: 30)."** This proves that He was not murdered, but died when the Holy Spirit instructed Him.

Jesus also fulfilled the Mosaic Law perfectly, which no other person had ever done. The Bible says that He was tempted in all points just as we are, but without sin because He solely relied on the Holy Spirit to guide Him during His earthly ministry (Hebrews 4: 15). This is exactly what God wants us to do to have victory over temptation and sin.

If we acccpt the New Covenant, which is faith in Jesus' finished work on the Cross for our salvation, then God looks upon us as being law keepers because our salvation is based on Jesus' perfection and not our own. In the Old Testament sacrificial system, when a sinner brought an animal to the High Priest to be slaughtered, *the High Priest would inspect the sacrificial animal and not the sinner.* That animal had to be perfect, because it had to represent Jesus, the Messiah.

But, as already mentioned, the blood of the animal sacrifice could only cover sin, not take it away like the precious blood of Jesus. Hebrews 10: 4 says, **"For it is not possible that the blood of bulls and goats should take away sins."** Then, Hebrews 10: 11 states, **"And every Priest stands daily ministering and offering oftentimes the same sacrifices, *which can never take away sins* (My italics)."** But John 1: 29 says, **"...Behold, the Lamb of God, which takes *away* the sin of the**

world (My italics)**.”**

Because Jesus fulfilled the Old Covenant, we no longer have to bring an innocent animal to be slaughtered for our transgressions. We only need to repent and place our faith in Jesus' sacrifice on our behalf. 1 John 1: 9 says that **“If we confess our sins, He is faithful and just to forgive us our sins and cleanse us of all unrighteousness.”** God desires for every person to make it to Heaven on day and that is why He makes His plan of redemption simple to understand and easy to accept. Wouldn't you agree that we are under a much better covenant today?

Chapter Six

STRANGE FIRE, A NEW CART & POLLUTION OF IDOLS

The title of this chapter encompasses three different, yet similar, subjects. All of them are indicative of religion, which attempts to reach God outside of Jesus and the Cross. Please remember that Jesus Christ is the source of salvation and the Cross is the means by which it was attained, thereby, allowing the Holy Spirit to lead us into a victorious life that is pleasing to God. Any other way is not accepted by God.

The Law of Moses given by God to instruct the Children of Israel was extremely precise and was expected to be followed flawlessly. Why? Is it because God is a controlling tyrant who wants to makes slaves of His people? No, not at all. Besides the fact that the Mosaic Law was to define sin, it also foreshadowed the coming Redeemer. God, in His mercy, wanted His chosen people to recognize the Saviour and to know without a shadow of a doubt when He would arrive.

The problem was that the Jewish people were looking for a handsome king, who had great power and would free them from Roman oppression and then set up His kingdom. They were not expecting a humble servant who began His ministry by riding on the back of a donkey. But God revealed to them almost 500 years before in Zechariah 9: 9, **"Rejoice greatly, O daughter of Zion; shout, O daughter of Jerusalem: behold, your King comes unto you: He is just, and having salvation; lowly, and riding upon an ass, and upon a colt the foal of an ass."** This prophecy of Zechariah came to fulfillment as recorded in Matthew 21: 5, where it says, **"Tell ye daughter of Sion, Behold, your King comes unto you, meek, and sitting upon an ass, and a colt the foal of an ass."**

And 800 years before the birth of Christ, Isaiah prophesied, **"For He shall grow up before Him as a tender plant, and as a root out of dry ground: He has no form nor comeliness; and when we shall see Him, there is no beauty that we should desire Him** (Isaiah 53: 2).**"** The religious Jews studied the Old Testament Scriptures diligently and should have known that Jesus was indeed the Messiah. But, as you will see in a future chapter, they treasured the religion created out of the Mosaic Law more than God's plan of redemption.

At His second coming, Jesus will finally come as the **"KING OF KINGS AND LORD OF LORDS** (Revelation 19: 15)**"** and will set up His earthly Kingdom. Matthew 24: 30 states, **"...and they shall see the Son of Man coming in the clouds of Heaven with power and great glory."** Jesus' second coming is also given in a vision by John in Revelation 19: 11 where it says, **"And I saw Heaven opened, and behold a white horse; and He Who sat upon him was called Faithful and True, and in righteousness He does judge and make war. His eyes were as a flame of fire and on His head were many crowns... and His name is called The Word of God."**

So, God had a reason for the meticulous instructions for Moses concerning the Law and the sacrificial system. As already stated, the entire structure of the Tabernacle of the Congregation typified Jesus. We did not go into great detail in the last chapter, but even the colors used to weave the Veil of the Temple, the animal skins layered over the Holy Place and the hardware fashioned of silver and used to hold the Tabernacle together represented Jesus Christ and His redemptive work.

During the time of Moses, his brother, Aaron was appointed by God as the first High Priest. Aaron's sons were consecrated as priests to assist with the animal sacrifices and the Tribe of Levi was chosen by God to take care of the Tabernacle. But, once Jesus died on the Cross, the office of the priesthood, as well as, the animal sacrifices would no longer be needed. As previously mentioned, Jesus was the very last High Priest because the moment that He died on the Cross, the heavy four inch Veil of the Temple was torn completely in two, showing that we have access directly to God through Jesus. Hebrews 4: 14 , 16 states, **"Seeing then that we have a Great High Priest Who is passed into the Heavens, Jesus the Son of God, let us hold fast to our profession... Let us therefore come boldly into the throne of grace, that we may obtain mercy, and find grace to help in time of need."**

In the Book of Leviticus, we are acquainted with Nadab and Abihu, Aaron's priestly sons. Leviticus 10: 1 states, **"And Nadab and Abihu, the sons of Aaron, took either of them his censer, and put fire therein, and put incense thereon, and offered strange fire before the LORD, which He commanded them not."** Nadab and Abihu had fetched fire to place on the Altar of Incense housed inside of the Holy Place. But the fire that they offered did not come from the Brazen Altar, as God had instructed in Exodus 30: 1, 9. Therefore, God called it **"strange fire."**

The consequence for dismissing God's command was instantaneous and it was severe. Leviticus 10: 2 states, **"And there went out fire from the LORD, and devoured them, and they died before the LORD."** A fire of judgment came forth from the Ark of the Covenant, through the Veil of the Temple, and consumed them while they stood by the Altar of Incense. This may seem harsh, but the priests were held to a very high standard and were expected to understand the laws and the consequences for not obeying. I have no doubt that Aaron had trained his sons not to offer strange fire on the Altar of Incense. But, like Cain, they took it upon themselves to ignore God's command and do it their own way. Both offenses resulted in serious consequences.

They had been instructed that the fire must come from the Brazen Altar because that is where the sacrificial animal was burned. The fire represented God's judgment on the sinner. So, by Nadab and Abihu obtaining fire from a different source, they were disregarding Jesus' future death on the Cross, of which the whole ceremony of the sin offering represented.

How does this pertain to us today? Offering **"strange fire"** to the Lord would be placing our faith for eternal salvation in something else besides **"Jesus Christ and Him Crucified (1 Corinthians 2: 2)."** Salvation must come through Jesus and *only* through His death on the Cross. If we take His death on the Cross out of the equation, then Jesus was simply a good man who went around healing people and performing miracles. While those things were great, none of it saved anyone from the fires of Hell. Separating Jesus from the Cross is a gross offense to God and Nadab and Abihu paid dearly for it.

Now that we have dealt with **"strange fire"** and the gross consequences of ignoring God's strict commands, we will transition to the matter of **"a new cart."** Exodus 37: 1-9 describes the measurements of the Ark of the Covenant, as well as, the way that it was to be crafted. It was to be made with shittim wood, which was a strong, indestructible wood. The shittim wood was to be overlaid with gold. But, the most significant portion of the Ark, the Mercy Seat, was to be made using solid gold, as well as, the two Cherubim whose wings covered the Mercy Seat. The next page features an image of what the Ark of the Covenant might have looked like.

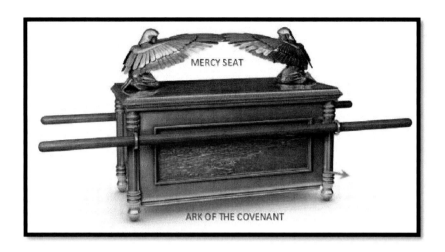

MERCY SEAT

ARK OF THE COVENANT

By far, the worst enemies of the Children of Israel were the Philistines. Once the Israelites finally crossed over to the Promised Land, the Philistines were there to challenge them around every corner. During the time of Samuel in 1141 B.C., the glory of the Lord departed from Israel when the Philistines captured the Ark of the Covenant (1 Samuel 4: 11, 22). The Philistines saw that it brought great power and victory to Israel, so they wanted to take that control away from the Children of Israel. They also had hoped that having the Ark in their camp would give them great power.

In 1 Samuel Chapter 5, the most fascinating thing happened when the Philistines brought the Ark of the Covenant into their camp. They brought the Ark into the house of Dagon, the Philistine fish god, and set it beside the statue of Dagon. The next morning, Dagon was face down before the Ark. The Philistines set the statue upright again, only to find it face down again the following morning, but this time with both the head and the palms severed. God was showing them that there is no false man-made god more powerful than Him, Jehovah God, the Creator of the Universe!

The Philistines thought that the Ark would bring them

blessings, but it only brought a great curse upon their land. God smote them and gave them skin tumors (1 Samuel 5: 6). They tried to pass the Ark off to other Philistine cities, but no one wanted it because they knew that the God of Israel would slay their people and destroy their cities. After seven months, the Philistines devised a plan to return the Ark to the Children of Israel. However, they decided to make some modifications by placing the Ark on a **"new cart,"** which contained offerings to the God of Israel. They sent two cows to bring it to Beth-shemesh and then watched from afar.

The people of Beth-shemesh recognized the Ark as it came toward them, but they did not understand that the Ark of the Covenant was meant to be hidden behind the Veil of the Temple and not in plain sight to be looked upon (Exodus 40: 3). As a result, many of the people of Beth-shemesh died. The remaining people wanted to rid themselves of the Ark, so they sent messengers to Kirjath-jiarim to come and fetch it and bring it into the house of Abinadab, where his son, Eleazar, took charge to keep it.

There is evidence that the Ark was neglected and remained in this area of Kirjath-jiarim for approximately twenty years, while the Children of Israel were mostly under the oppression of the Philistines. It remained there during the forty year reign of King Saul, Israel's first appointed King. And then when King David succeeded Saul, the Ark remained there for ten more years before it was brought to Jerusalem. From all accounts, in Psalms 132: 6, David discovered it in a field, neglected and abandoned for a grand total of seventy years.

After a great victory over the Philistines, King David consulted the elders of Israel, and *not the Lord*, concerning bringing the Ark of the Covenant back to Jerusalem. While David's motives were good, because the Ark certainly belonged in Jerusalem, he went about retrieving the Ark in the wrong way. Borrowing an idea from Israel's worst rival, David called for the

Ark to be returned on a **"new cart."** 2 Samuel 6: 3 states, **"And they set the Ark of God upon a new cart, and brought it out of the house of Abinadab that was in Gibeah: and Uzzah and Ahio, the sons of Abinadab, drove the new cart."**

The Mosaic Law stated that the priests must carry the Ark upon their shoulders using the wooden staves as leverage. They were warned that if they touched the actual Ark, they would instantly die (Numbers 4: 15). The priests were a type of Christ, as He would come to fulfill the office of the priesthood, but Israel chose to make a **"new cart,"** just as the Philistines had done seventy years prior. They would sorely regret it.

2 Samuel 6: 5 says, **"And David and all the house of Israel played before the LORD on all manner of instruments made of fir wood, even on harps, and on psalteries, and on timbrels, and on cornets and on cymbals."** David tried with all of his flesh to make this ceremony spectacular, but this was not what God wanted. He only cared that the Ark of the Covenant be treated as He had instructed Moses. Had David just conferred with God and not with man, this catastrophe would have been entirely avoided.

Then 2 Samuel 6: 6-7 states, **"And when they came to Nachon's threshingfloor, Uzzah put forth his hand to the Ark of God, and took hold of it; for the oxen shook it. And the anger of the LORD was kindled against Uzzah; and God smote him there for his error; and there he died by the Ark of God."** The **"new cart"** with the Ark sitting atop was being pulled by oxen, but when the oxen shook the cart, Uzzah was concerned that the Ark would fall. When he reached out to stabilize the Ark, it resulted in the immediate punishment of death. Uzzah probably thought that he was serving God by leading this elaborate ceremony, but God was not impressed in the least.

David finally came to his senses and consulted God on the matter of bringing the Ark back to Jerusalem. Three months later, the Ark of the Covenant was brought into Jerusalem the proper way. It was not long after that when God gave King David the specifications for the Temple, which Solomon would eventually build. David learned a hard lesson and Uzzah paid the price for the construction of a **"new cart."**

There are many **"new carts"** in today's modern churches as they attempt to "reinvent Christianity." I assure you that God is not pleased. If a church is not preaching about the great victory that Jesus won on the Cross when He defeated sin, death, Hell and Satan, then it is time to consult God for direction. While churches today are crawling with people and programs of every kind, what good does it do for a person to attend a church if it is not teaching them about Jesus and His finished work on the Cross? Be careful not to be associated with the **"new cart."** It only brings spiritual death.

Now, let's get to the final subject of this chapter concerning **"pollution of idols."** The word "pollution" certainly gives a negative connotation, as it should. The word "idol" is used many times in the Bible, often in reference to Israel. God had called the Israelites to be His chosen people, but they were surrounded by other nations, which idolized false gods. Unfortunately, the Children of Israel succumbed to these influences and were caught "whoring" after idols on many occasions.

This is a picture of the dilemma of man. Will he serve Jehovah God alone, or will he turn aside his devotion and worship idols? We can't do both. Matthew 6: 24 warns, **"No man can have two masters: for either he will hate the one, and love the other; or else he will hold to the one, and despise the other. You cannot serve God and mammon."**

In Exodus Chapter 20, God gives Moses the Ten Commandments. The very first commandment He gives is, **"I am the LORD your God, which have brought you out of Egypt,** out of the house of bondage. *You shall have no other gods before me* (My italics)." The very next commandment states, **"You shall not make unto yourself any graven image... You shall not bow down yourself to them, nor serve them** (Exodus 20: 4, 5)." Let's deal with each of these separately.

In Acts 15: 20, Paul exhorts believers to **"abstain from pollutions of idols."** When someone uses the word "idol," likely we picture a statue of some sort. This is partly true because there were countless statues of false gods in Old Testament times. Today, there are religions that have statues littering their churches and this should certainly be a red flag to anyone seeking a true relationship with God through Jesus Christ. God called the Israelites to break down the statues and the groves of idols when they conquered a land and its people. God is never in favor of statues which are idolized, prayed to, used for "miracles," or seen as talismans against evil.

1 John 5: 21 says, **"Little children, keep yourself from idols."** Here, it is not necessarily referring to heathen idols, but anything that we put before our relationship with God. God says *"You shall have no other gods before me."* If we put our own selves, our work, our spouse, our children, recreation, or even our service before our relationship with God, then it plain and simply becomes an idol.

We must seek God each and every day for His will to be done in our lives. This can only happen when we die to our own flesh, look to what Jesus accomplished on the Cross, yield our lives to the Lord and allow the Holy Spirit to guide and lead us. When we do this, great things will happen for the Kingdom of God, but it won't be for our glory, it will all be for the Glory of God.

Luke 9: 23 explains, **"And He** (Jesus) **said unto them all, If any man will come after Me, let him deny himself, and take up his cross daily, and follow Me."** And Proverbs 3: 5-6 says, **"Trust in the LORD with all your heart; and lean not unto** your own understanding. **In all your ways acknowledge Him, and He shall direct your paths."**

In Oswald Chambers *My Utmost for His Highest* February 10th devotional, it reads[9]:

> Is your mind focused on the face of an idol? Is the idol yourself? Is it your work? Is it your idea of what a servant should be, or maybe your experience of salvation and sanctification? If so, then your ability to see God is blinded. You will be powerless when faced with difficulties and will be forced to endure in darkness. If your power to see has been blinded, don't look back on your own experiences, but look to God. It is God you need. Go beyond yourself and away from faces of your idols and away from everything else that has been blinding your thinking..."

God has not changed, despite the fact that we are under a much better covenant than of the Old Testament times. Hebrews 13: 8, 9 states, **"Jesus Christ, the same yesterday, and today and forever. Be not carried about with divers and strange doctrines. For it is a good thing that the heart be established with Grace, not with meats, which have not profited them who have been occupied therein."** The only thing that has changed is that Jesus came to fulfill the Old Covenant. He did so perfectly, and now we are to look back at what He accomplished, instead of looking forward to it as the Old Testament believers.

------

[9] *My Utmost for His Highest,* Oswald Chambers, 1935 Original publication, revised in 1992, Discovery House Publishers, February 10th devotion

God only wants our faith in Jesus Christ and He is not impressed with our own efforts and religious pageantry. This is proven with the story of Nadab and Abihu's **"strange fire,"** and Uzzah, who took hold of the **"new cart."** Both of these incidents resulted in immediate death. These accounts given in the Bible are lessons from God that we should not follow their lead. For us, it would not mean instant physical death because we are under the New Covenant. However, it will mean a spiritual death, or a deep separation from God, when we choose to go outside of the Cross of Jesus Christ or dismiss it all together.

Chapter Seven

A GENERATION OF VIPERS

Why don't we set the stage for this chapter with a quick review of some of the information already presented, followed with a timeline of the political and spiritual influences during the time of Jesus. We have already established that God had chosen a race of people to bring forth the Redeemer, through the lineage of Abraham, Isaac and Jacob. God made a covenant with the Israelites and gave them the land of Canaan, which became known as Israel.

When Jacob was patriarch, the Israelites fled to Egypt to escape the famine in Canaan. This resulted in them spending 400 years under Egyptian bondage. Egypt was the dominant world superpower during this period of history. *In the Bible, Egypt represents the world, and Pharaoh represents Satan.* The plight of the Israelites is so significant because God uses their highs and lows to show us how to live victoriously for Him.

We have also covered the 613 Mosaic Laws handed down by God to define sin. God implemented the sacrificial system to give the nation of Israel a means to cover sin and also to point them to the coming Messiah. He established the office of the High Priest and the priesthood to offer the animal sacrifices, as well as, the tribe of Levi to take care of the Tabernacle, and later the Temple.

God had originally chosen the Israelites to rule all nations and He had committed the scepter of world power into her hands (Deuteronomy 32: 8). But, as a consequence of Israel's continual idolatry, He took that power from her and placed it into the hands of Nebuchadnezzar and then to his successors, where it still remains today.

Because of Israel's backsliding, in 607 B.C., God allowed their Temple to be destroyed and for them to be taken captive into Babylon, where King Nebuchadnezzar ruled. Babylon was eventually conquered by Medo-Persia and a new Temple was built during this time. Israel became a vassal state under Medo-Persian rule, which lasted from 540 B.C. until 332 B.C.

Around 332 B.C., the Medes and Persians were conquered by the Greeks under the command of Alexander the Great. Grecian rule lasted until 186 B.C., when the power shifted as the Roman Empire took control of the majority of the known world and ruled with an iron fist.

Daniel 2: 40, describes the Roman Empire by stating, **"And the fourth Kingdom shall be strong as iron: Forasmuch as iron breaks into pieces and subdues all things: and as iron that breaks all these, shall it break in pieces and bruise."** History reveals the brutality of the Roman Empire, which confirms the accuracy of this prophecy given by Daniel.

Then in Daniel 7: 7, he relates his vision concerning the Roman Empire when he says, **"After this I saw in the night visions, and behold a fourth beast, dreadful and terrible, and strong exceedingly and it had great iron teeth: it devoured and broke in pieces, and stamped the residue with the feet of it; and was diverse from all the beasts that were before it…"**

The powerful Roman Empire was still in control during the time of Jesus. Israel was a vassal state and the Jews were allowed to practice their religion, as long as they recognized the Roman caesar, or emperor, as "god on Earth." Kenneth Wuest, in an article concerning the Roman Empire's Cult of Caesar, states:

> The Empire, made up of many widely different peoples with their own distinct languages, customs, and religions, was held together not merely by one central

ruling power at Rome, which was supported by the military power of its legions, but also and probably more efficiently so, by the universal religion of emperor-worship. Political and military ties are strong, but religious ties are stronger. Rome knew this and guarded jealously its Cult of the Caesar. *Its policy was to allow its subjects to retain their own religions as long as they accepted Emperor-worship in addition to their own system of belief* (My italics). [10]

By the Jews obeying this Roman rule, they were breaking God's commandment of **"Thou shall have no other gods before me (Exodus 23: 3)."** But, as you will see, the hierarchy of Israel was much more concerned with worldly aspirations than with true devotion to God.

The Old Testament portion of the Bible was very clear, giving the precise time that the Messiah would appear and even predicted, almost to the day, His crucifixion (Daniel 9: 24-25). The Scriptures were very specific that the Messiah would be born of a virgin (Isaiah 7: 14) and that He would be born in Bethlehem (Micah 5: 2). In other words, the religious Jews, who knew the Scriptures impeccably, should have been watching closely for the appearance of the Messiah. Unfortunately they became wrapped up in climbing the hierarchal ladder of Judaism and were more concerned about their place and position.

When Jesus made His public debut as the Messiah, the Pharisees and Sadducees, as well as, the High Priests, were

---

[10] Kenneth Wuest, *World Studies in the Greek New Testament*, Volume III, Eardmans Publishing, 1940, pages 21-25

threatened by this man who claimed that He was the Son of God. Also, the Roman caesar, who already ruled over the Jewish hierarchy, would not tolerate this imperial rivalry. The term *kurios,* meaning "Lord," was used as the divine title of the emperor, but it was also an official title of the Lord Jesus Christ. Another title given the emperor was *basileus* or "king," which is certainly a title given to Jesus, the **"King of kings."** Then the term *theos,* meaning "god," and *huios theou,* meaning "son of god," were both titles of the Roman emperor. Also, the term used by the Roman emperor was *archiereus,* meaning "High Priest."[11] The emperors were referred to as "Pontifex Maximus," meaning "High Priest." Of course, Jesus was referenced as God, Son of God and also as the great High Priest by Paul in Hebrews 4: 14. Kenneth Wuest writes:

> Here was Heaven's King coming to dispute the claims and positions of the caesar who arrogated to himself the title of "lord," and who was worshiped as a god. No wonder that Herod and the Jews were agitated at this news (Matthew 2: 1–8), the former because of the imperialistic challenge by which would present new problems of administration to him in addition to the ones he already had in connection with troublesome Israel, the latter because, entrenched in their ecclesiastical sin, they did not want to be deprived of their lucrative positions.[12]

---

[11] Kenneth Wuest, *World Studies in the Greek New Testament*, Volume III, Eardmans Publishing, 1940, pages 21-25
[12] Kenneth Wuest, *World Studies in the Greek New Testament*, Volume III, Eardmans Publishing, 1940, page 23

It was their *"lucrative positions"* and *"ecclesiastical sin"* that caused these religious Jews to hate Jesus with such vehemence that they would repeatedly shout **"Crucify Him!"**

Kenneth Wuest goes on to state in the same article:

> But not only did the emperor have the titles of Lord, son of God, god, overseer, and king, all of which were titles of our Lord also, but he was given the title *soter,* "saviour."
>
> At least eight of the emperors carried the title 'saviour of the world.' They were hailed as the saviours of the people. For the most part, the Roman world was well governed and policed, Roman law was administered in equity, the Roman roads caused travel and commerce to flourish, the Roman peace made living conditions bearable and in some instances pleasant. Thus the emperors were the world-saviours. Now comes Christianity with its imperialistic announcement, 'For unto you is born this day in the city of David a Saviour, which is Christ the Lord (Luke 2:11).' But this Saviour's name was Jesus, the one who would save them from the sins which they loved and from which they did not want to be separated. What motive would they have been transferring their allegiance from a world-saviour who gave them the comforts of life and at the same time allows them to go on in their sin, to the Lord Jesus, especially when allegiance to this new Saviour could very well result in their crucifixion by Rome?[13]

---

[13] Kenneth Wuest, *World Studies in the Greek New Testament*, Volume III, Eardmans Publishing, 1940, pages 26-27

The Roman caesar had a deep desire to have control and to be deified and the High Priests, Sadducees and Pharisees wanted to secure high positions of power; but Jesus made them face their sinful and wicked desires. As Wuest states, *"...Jesus, the one who would save them from the sins which they loved and from which they did not want to be separated."* How depraved to love their sins so much that they would reject the one Man who could wash away their scarlet sins and make them **"white as snow** (Isaiah 1: 18).**"**

God warns us in 1 John 2: 15-17, where it says, **"Love not the world, neither the things that are in the world. If any man love the world, the love of the Father is not in him. For all that is in the world, the lust of the flesh, and the lust of the eyes, and the pride of life, is not of the Father, but is of the world. And the world passes away, and the lust thereof: but he who does the will of God abides forever."** What a promise! There are many more Scriptures that echo God's promises of eternal life for those who are willing to die to self and follow God's will.

Immediately after Jesus made His triumphant entrance into Jerusalem to begin His earthly ministry, His very first stop was to cleanse the Temple. Unfortunately, the religious leaders had made it into a place of merchandise. Matthew 21: 12-13 states, **"And Jesus went into the Temple of God, and cast out all who sold and bought in the Temple, and overthrew the tables of the moneychangers, and the seats of them who sold doves. And said unto them, It is written, My house shall be called a house of prayer; but you have made it a den of thieves."**

The religious leaders tried on many occasions to trick Jesus, but each time, He made them look like fools instead. This, of course, angered them greatly. They were terrified that if the people accepted Jesus as the Messiah, they would lose their powerful positions.

What did Jesus think of these religious Jews? Jesus called the Pharisees and Sadducees **"hypocrites"** over seventeen times in the Bible. He referred to them as "a generation of vipers (Matthew 3: 7, 12: 34, 23: 33; Luke 3: 7); and "whited sepulchers, which indeed appear beautiful outward, but are full of dead men's bones (Matthew 23: 27)."

In Matthew 23: 1-4, Jesus warns the multitude of people saying, "The Scribes and the Pharisees sit in Moses' seat: All therefore whatsoever they bid you observe, that observe and do; but do not ye after their works: for they say, and do not do. For they bind heavy burdens and grievous to be borne, and lay them on men's shoulders; but they themselves will not move them with one of their fingers." Jesus exposes that the religious leaders do not "practice what they preach" and also that they had doubled the Law of Moses. They had taken what was sacred and fabricated man-made demands on the Jewish people. This is indicative of religious man, taking God's commands and twisting them to meet man's idea of righteousness.

Jesus goes on to say, "But all their works they do for to be seen of men... And love the uppermost rooms at feasts, and the chief seats in the synagogues, and greeting in the markets, and to be called of men, Rabbi, Rabbi." When you really boil it down, this is what the religious leaders truly desired. It was to impress other men and get special treatment. Jesus exposed what was truly in their wicked hearts and they vehemently despised Him for it.

In Luke 22: 24-27, there is an account after the Lord's Supper where the Apostles were arguing over place and position in the Kingdom of God. It says, "And there was also a strife among them, which of them should be accounted the greatest. And He said unto them, The kings of the Gentiles exercise lordship over them; and they that exercise authority upon them are called benefactors. But ye shall not be so: but he who is greatest among you, let him be as the younger; and he who is chief, as he who does serve. For whether is greater, he who sits at meat, or he who serves? But I am among you as He who serves." Jesus set His apostles straight about hierarchy and indicated that no one person would be greater than another.

Also, Jesus said in Matthew 23: 8- 9, **"But you are not to be called Rabbi: for one is your Master, even Christ; and all you are brethren. And call no man your father upon the earth: for one is your Father, which is in Heaven."** The Scripture says **"all you are brethren,"** meaning that no one believer is to be ranked higher than another.

The truth is that religion and the desire for power are what nailed Jesus to the Cross. God, in His foreknowledge, knew that His chosen Messiah would be rejected and this is why He provided the sacrificial system to point to the coming Saviour. From all accounts, the religious leaders were aware that Jesus was the Son of God. They had the Old Testament Scriptures committed to memory and could not deny the miracles that Jesus performed, or His supernatural knowledge and wisdom.

But, again, they chose their own version of righteousness, instead of admitting that Jesus was the Son of God and the Messiah. As a result, it has caused the Jewish race great persecution down through the ages. Had they simply accepted Jesus as their Saviour, He would have set up His Kingdom right then and there and we would have peace on Earth today. The Jewish race would have ruled over the whole world, but they forfeited that right when they rejected the Son of God.

Now, we must wait for Jesus' second coming, when He will come with great power and glory. He will also defeat the Antichrist and establish His Kingdom on Earth for 1,000 years. After the millennial reign of Jesus, Heaven will come down to Earth and we will live without Satan and sin in the Kingdom of God, just as He first intended when He created mankind (Revelation Chapters 19-22).

These Jewish religious leaders parallel religious hierarchy today, who believe that their place and position earn them some kind of special grace from God. Their pomp and ceremony may look beautiful on the outside, with their elaborate apparel and ornate altars, but God does not require these spectacles. None of this impresses God in the least. Matthew 23: 12 explains, **"And whosoever shall exalt himself shall be abased** (degraded)**; and he that shall humble himself shall be exalted."**

Chapter Eight

HIGH ON RELIGION

When someone is "high," it gives the implication of the person feeling exhilarated and euphoric. Religion seems to have the exact same effect on man. Anyone who has done a good deed or has gone out of the way to attend a church service will tell you that it feels really good afterward. There is joy and the feeling that we have earned something as a result. We feel that God must be pleased by our actions. Well, is He?

The answer lies in our motives. Are we doing these things to glorify God or is it to magnify *ourselves*? Do we make sure that others see our deeds so that they will think we are "good" or "holy?" Do we think that by doing good works, we can earn salvation or special graces from God outside of Jesus' finished work on the Cross? This is a topic we have touched on already in the chapter concerning the tree of the knowledge of good and evil, but it is a very important one and deserves a chapter all its own.

There is the misconception that the euphoria we feel is confirmation from God that we have done well in His eyes. But, remember, the only thing that pleases God is *faith in Jesus' once and for all sacrifice.* When we introduce others to the Gospel of Jesus Christ, God is certainly pleased, despite the fact that it earns us nothing. We tell others about Jesus because we want them to know the truth and have eternal life. The preaching of the Gospel is the only way that others can hear the good news that, although we were born in sin, Jesus Christ, the Son of God, died on the Cross to save our souls from an eternal separation from God.

Romans 10: 14-15, 17 states, **"How then shall they call on Him in Whom they have not believed? And how shall they believe in Him of Whom they have not heard? And how shall they hear without a preacher? And how shall they preach, except they be sent? How beautiful are the feet of them who preach the Gospel of peace, and bring glad tidings of good things...** *So then faith comes by hearing, and hearing by the Word of God* (My italics).**"

2 Timothy 3: 1-7 sums up the condition of mankind in the last days. Paul states, **"This know also, that in the last days perilous times shall come. For men shall be lovers of their own selves, covetous, boasters, proud, blasphemers, disobedient to parents, unthankful, unholy, without natural affection, trucebreakers, false accusers, incontinent, fierce, despisers of those who are good, traitors, heady, high-minded, lovers of pleasures more than lovers of God; Having a form of godliness, but denying the power thereof...Ever learning, and never able to come to the knowledge of truth: men of corrupt minds, reprobate concerning the Faith."** You will find many people today who have **"a form of godliness,"** but most of the time their motives are to feel good about themselves and to convince others that they are holy.

It is important to understand that our motives will one day be judged by God. So, if we are performing works to gain favor from God or to look holy to our fellow man, then God says that those deeds will be tried by fire. 1 Corinthians 3: 11-13 states concerning our works and motives, **"For other foundation can no man lay than that is laid, which is Jesus Christ. Now if any man build upon this foundation gold, silver, precious stones, wood, hay stubble; Every man's work shall be made manifest: for the day shall declare it, because it shall be revealed by fire; and the fire shall try every man's work of what sort it is."**

We should serve God because we love Him and have a burden for others to hear the truth of the Gospel. Inevitably, placing God first in our lives will produce the **"fruit of the spirit,"** [14] which is pleasing to Him. But, we cannot earn anything from God and Ephesians 2: 8-9 proves this when it states, **"For by Grace are you saved through Faith; and that not of yourselves: it is the Gift of God: Not of works, lest any man should boast."** Salvation is a free **"Gift of God,"** which means that it cannot be bought or earned.

We cannot hide what is in our hearts from God. What happens when we perform works for God with the wrong motives? *Self-effort produces an ugly thing called "self-righteousness."* If you have ever encountered a self-righteous person, you know that they are so full of themselves that the Holy Spirit has no room to move in their lives.

The religious leaders of Israel were full of indignation and self-righteousness and we know how Jesus felt about them. Jesus said in Matthew 5: 20, **"For I say unto you, Except that your righteousness shall exceed the righteousness of the Scribes and the Pharisees** (which was self-righteousness)**, you shall in no case enter into the Kingdom of Heaven** (My notes in parentheses)**."**

What does God want? He desires a humble and contrite heart, empty of the flesh and welcome to the Holy Spirit. This is what truly produces righteousness that is worthy of eternity in Heaven. Isaiah 57: 15 states **"For thus saith the high and lofty One Who inhabits eternity, Whose Name is Holy; I dwell in the high and holy place, with him also that is of a contrite and**

---

[14] Galatians 5:22, **"By the fruit of the Spirit is love, joy, peace, long-suffering, gentleness, goodness, faith."**

humble spirit, to revive the spirit of the humble, and to revive the heart of the contrite ones."

The word "contrite," denotes a broken and repentant heart. It is indicative or someone who is grateful for their salvation, knowing that, in and of themselves, they did nothing to earn it. Psalms 34: 18 says, **"The LORD is nigh unto them that are of a broken heart; and saves such as be of a contrite spirit."** And Psalms 51: 17 states, **"The sacrifices of God are a broken spirit: a broken and contrite heart, O God, thou will not despise."**

This kind of repentant heart produces the proper righteousness for salvation and is the polar opposite of efforts by the flesh to obtain salvation or God's grace. As stated, these fleshly efforts produce self-righteousness, which give the individual performing them a "high," but they are actually an abomination unto God. We cannot earn what Jesus already paid for when He went to the Cross. To God, when we do such, we are essentially saying that what Jesus accomplished was not sufficient for our salvation. 2 Corinthians 5: 7 reminds us that **"We walk by faith, not by sight,"** *or by feelings.*

THE BIG THREE

While we couldn't possibly explore every single religion in the world today, seeing that there are over 4300[15], I felt that it would be an interesting study to highlight some of the more prominent religions and their belief systems. My goal is to present facts and at times compare them to what has already been offered as God's blueprint for eternal life in Heaven.

If you would go out on the streets and interview 1,000 people concerning the path to eternal life, likely the large majority of them would say that there are many paths to Heaven. But, Jesus discredits that theory in Matthew 7: 13-14, when He says, **"Enter you in at the strait gate: for wide is the gate, and broad is the way, that leads to destruction, and many there be which go in thereat: Because strait is the gate, and narrow is the way, which leads unto life, and few there be that find it."**

The many different paths to Heaven are the **"wide"** and **"broad"** gate which Jesus speaks of and He specifically says that this way **"leads to destruction."** However, He says that the **"strait"** and **"narrow"** gate **"leads unto life,"** meaning eternal life. Remember that **"the gate"** was the only entrance into the Tabernacle of the Congregation and it represented Jesus as the only avenue into Heaven.

---

[15] https://www.reference.com/world-view/total-number-religions-world-ff89ae17c6068514

There is the collective idea that all religions contain the same basic truth, but they only present the truth in diverse ways. According to this view, God is placed at the tip-top of a mountain and there are many different paths that lead up to Him. There is just one problem: *all religions cannot be true.* Why? Because they are all diverse and many claim to be the only exclusive path to salvation, so much so, that they will kill those who will not join their ranks.

In another chapter, we will reveal where one can find objective truth because many religions contain some element of truth, which can be confusing. However, that does not mean that the entire religion is true just because there is some element of truth intertwined. We must be careful of any belief system that contains only partial truth.

Jesus told His followers multiple times, **"Beware of the leaven of the Pharisees and the Sadducees** (Matthew 16: 6, 11, 12, Mark 8: 15; Luke 12: 1)."** Galatians 5: 9 says, **"a little leaven leavens the whole lump."** Unleavened bread was used in Old Testament times by the Children of Israel for certain feasts. Leaven would function in the same manner that yeast would, to make dough rise. Jesus uses the word "leaven" to reveal that even if a tiny speck of leaven were to get into the dough, it would eventually cause the whole ball of dough to rise.

In the Bible, "leaven" is often used to signify sin and corruption. So, if a religion is teaching *mostly* truth, but not all truth according to the Word of God, even a little untruth is going to cause the **"whole lump,"** or congregation, to be affected. If a person consumed just a little bit of poison each day, eventually, as the poison builds up in the body, it will cause weakness, sickness and eventually death.

We will first take a look at the big three monotheistic religions today: Christianity, Islam and Judaism. Monotheistic religions believe that there is only one God. Christianity is the only one that acknowledges Jesus as divine, but even some sects of what is considered Christianity today worship **"another Jesus (2 Corinthians 11: 3-4),"** which we covered in an earlier chapter. Their "Jesus" did not completely pay for our salvation, because they require their faithful to perform certain works to obtain eternal life in Heaven.

CHRISTIANITY

What we will find when we break down the term "Christianity" is that it encompasses several religions of its own, including Roman Catholicism, Protestantism, Orthodox and Anglicans or Episcopalians. While we will deal briefly with each of these, the beliefs of the Roman Catholic Church will be uncovered in the next chapter.

Because today's Christianity includes many religions that were created out of the true Church formed after Jesus' ascension, these religions have added their man-made doctrines and creeds to God's simple plan of salvation. Just as the Pharisees and Sadducees took the Mosaic Law and doubled its rules, these religions have done just the same.

Jesus said in Matthew 15: 8-9, **"This people draw near unto Me with their mouth, and honor Me with their lips; but their heart is far from Me. But in vain they do worship Me, teaching for doctrines the commandments of men."** And Paul said in Colossians 2: 8, **"Beware lest any man spoil you through philosophy and vain deceit, after the tradition of men, after the rudiments of the world, and not after Christ."**

Let's determine what the biblical term "Christian" means. A "Christian" can be defined as a follower of Christ. Just to clarify, true Christianity, which developed with the Early Church, was never intended to be a religion at all. *Christianity is based on the belief that Jesus Christ died on the Cross to free the world of sin and death brought about by the Fall of Man through Satan.* True Christianity can better be described as a "relationship with God" and not a religion.

The first mention in the Bible of **"Christians"** is found in Acts 11: 26 and speaks of those people who had accepted Jesus' death on the Cross for their salvation. These people did not have to perform certain ceremonies or rituals to become Christians. Their one and only requirement was simply to *believe* that Jesus was the Son of God and that He came to save them from the penalty of sin. Most of these people were water baptized, but the act of baptism was not what saved them (1 Peter 3: 21). On the contrary, their salvation was based on the acceptance of the Cross, with their baptism in water following as a public proclamation of being identified with the death and resurrection of Jesus Christ.

After Jesus' ascension, He commanded His disciples to go out into the whole world and preach the Gospel after they were baptized in the Holy Spirit on the day of Pentecost (Luke 16: 15). Because of the great persecution from the religious Jews, as well as, the Roman hierarchy, the followers of Christ were scattered all over the known world and likewise, the Gospel of Jesus Christ was spread.

In 313 A.D., the Roman Emperor Constantine issued the Edict of Milan, which gave Christians the opportunity to worship within the Roman Empire as they desired, without fear of persecution. Some Christians of the Early Church, tired of persecution, accepted this offer and this acceptance is what united the pagan Roman practice of emperor worship with true Christianity.

The result of Constantine's proposal eventually became the religion of Roman Catholicism. Because Christianity was recognized alongside paganism, Constantine set himself up as the leader of this new church. He combined church and state and called himself the "Vicar of Christ," which is still the official title of the pope of the Roman Catholic Church to this day. Constantine also held the title of Pontifex Maximus, meaning High Priest, which is another identical title used of the pope of Rome today. *So over time, the Roman emperor eventually transformed into the pope of the Roman Catholic Church.*

Under Constantine, the new amalgam of Christianity and pagan Roman traditions combined to form a universal church, which was entitled the "Catholic Church," because the word "catholic" means "universal." Eventually, the hierarchy began to claim that the Roman Catholic Church was the one and only true church and that there was no salvation outside of it. From an approved Roman Catholic publication, Kenneth D. Whitehead explains the position of the Church of Rome when it comes to her title and her exclusivity:

> The proper name of the Church, then, is the Catholic Church. It is not ever called "the Christian Church," either... As mentioned in the Acts of the Apostles, it is true that the followers of Christ early on became known as "Christians" (Acts 11: 26). The name Christian, however, was never commonly applied to the Catholic Church herself.

> The *Catechism of the Catholic Church* in our own day has concisely summed up all the reasons why the name of the Church of Christ has been the Catholic Church: 'The Church is catholic,' the Catechism teaches, '[because] she proclaims the fullness of the faith. She bears in herself and administers the totality of the means of salvation. She is sent out to all peoples. She speaks to all men. She encompasses all times. She is missionary of her

very nature (*Catechism of the Catholic Church*, 868).'[16]

In 313 A.D., when Emperor Constantine married church and state with the Edict of Milan, he claimed to convert to Christianity, but it was strictly for political reasons. *Christianity Today* describes Constantine's motives in their "Christian History" section online, where it states:

> Historians now debate whether 'the first Christian emperor' was a Christian at all. Some think him an unprincipled power seeker. What religion he had, many argue, was at *best a blend of paganism and Christianity for purely political purposes...* Certainly, Constantine held to ideals we no longer share. He knew nothing of religion without politics or politics without religion (My italics).[17]

We already confirmed that the Roman Empire was brutal by nature and was described in Daniel 7: 7 as **"dreadful and terrible, and strong exceedingly and it had great iron teeth: it devoured and broke in pieces, and stamped the residue with the feet of it; and was diverse from all the beasts that were before it..."** This description was spot on, because Rome persecuted and killed those who would not bow down to her political and religious system. True Christians could not worship both the Roman emperor and the one true God and they paid dearly in the many inquisitions hurled at them by Rome.

---

[16] Kenneth D. Whitehead, *The Catholic Answer*, May/June 1996 Published by Our Sunday Visitor, Inc., Huntington, IN
[17] http://www.christianitytoday.com/history/people/rulers/constantine.html

The result of Emperor Constantine's Edict was that thousands of pagans joined the state church in order to gain the special advantages and favors that went with such membership, with no intentions of ever becoming true Christians. They came into Constantine's universal church in far greater numbers than could be assimilated and instructed properly. Having been accustomed to the more elaborate pagan rituals, they were not satisfied with simple Christian worship, so they began to introduce their heathen beliefs and practices.

Gradually, through the neglect of the Word of God and the lack of diligence of the people concerning the truth, more and more pagan practices were introduced until the church became more pagan than it was Christian. Many of the heathen temples were taken over by the church and rededicated as Christian churches. Over time, there was found an exquisitely appareled priesthood, elaborate rituals, statues, incense, holy water, monks and nuns, Purgatory, and the most damning was the belief that salvation was now to be achieved by works rather than by faith in the finished work of Jesus on the Cross. As a result, the church in Rome, and the churches throughout the Roman Empire, ceased to be the church created by Jesus Christ and carried on by His apostles and disciples, but became what Jesus despised most, a religious institution.

Of course, there remained a small remnant who maintained the true Christian faith of the Early Church. Many of these Christians fled to Europe and Asia Minor into the mountains to escape from the persecution. These people were the true Church, instituted by Jesus Christ, and they looked upon Rome's apostate religion as anti-Christ. Some of these individuals were the Waldenses and Albigenses, who were forerunners to the great reformers who succeeded them. They were true Christians, defending their faith even unto death. Jesus said in John 16: 2-4, **"...yea, the time comes that whosoever kills you will think he** does God a service. And these things they will do unto you, because they have not known the Father, nor Me..."

As time went by, the religion that Constantine had created with his universal, "catholic," church began to gain great power and wealth. All of the kings and people of the Earth were to submit and bow down to the emperor, who eventually became known as the pope around 606 A.D.

During the Dark Ages, the greed and control of the Roman Catholic Church became so obtrusive that many of their own priests were fed up and called for reform within the Church. These men became known as "reformers," and one in particular, Martin Luther, sparked the Reformation, which began in 1517 A.D. As a result of Martin Luther nailing his 95 Theses to the door of the Wittenberg Chapel on October 31, 1517, many weary people, who had been held in the iron vice of Rome, began to see the religion for what it really was, an imposter to the true Church of Jesus Christ.

You see, God never intended people to be in bondage to a religion, but the Roman Catholic Church took what was developed out of the Early Church, added her spin on how to reach Heaven, and forced people to abide by her rules. And because she was the political ruling force, she was able to enforce her political and spiritual laws. Rome kept the Word of God from the people, chained the Bible to the pulpit and claimed that only the hierarchy could interpret Scripture. The people were enslaved, dumbed down and threatened with torture and death for coming against "Mother Church."

Those who escaped Rome's oppression were labeled as "Protestants" by Pope Paul III. Roman Catholics often attempt to represent Protestantism as something comparatively new and as having originated with Martin Luther and other reformers in the 16th century. While we certainly owe some gratitude to the leaders of the Reformation, who exposed the hypocrisy of Rome and brought the Word of God and the Gospel back into the light, the basic principles of doctrine taught by the reformers can be traced back to the 1st century Christian Church.

"Protestantism," as it emerged in the 16th century, was not the beginning of something new, but a return to biblical Christianity and to the simplicity of the true Gospel, which the Roman Catholic Church had perverted and complicated. Over time, Protestantism led to the formation of various churches, some of which are still around today. Some include: the Anglican Church of England; the Episcopal Church of America; the Methodist Church; the Baptist Church; the Presbyterian Church and the Pentecostal Church.

The Anglican Church, originally known as the Church of England, was formed out of Henry VIII's desire for an annulment of his marriage to Catherine of Aragon, which Pope Clement VII would not allow. As a result, King Henry broke from the Roman Catholic Church and created what became the Anglican Church in the 16th century. The belief system of the Anglican Church is similar to that of the Roman Catholic Church, but with some Protestantism also mixed in, because the forming of this Church took place around the same time as the Reformation. The Anglican Communion has 80 million members worldwide in thirty-eight different church organizations, including the Episcopal Church of America. The Archbishop of Canterbury is the recognized spiritual head of the church, though each church organization is self-governing under its own archbishop.[18]

The other denominations mentioned above were each created some time after the Reformation of 1517 and all refer to their members as "Christians." Each one of these denominations

---

[18] https://www.gotquestions.org/Anglicans.html

believes that salvation is by the blood of Jesus alone. However, they all have their own distinct ideas concerning certain aspects of Christianity.

I will admit that Protestantism today is a tangled web of bickering denominations. Anytime man begins making his own spiritual rules, he reverts back to law, which cannot coexist with God's free gift of grace in Jesus Christ. Many Protestant denominations have done just this and they are abrogating the finished work of Jesus Christ on the Cross. Over time, Satan had his way and these denominations have become more like the world and less like the true Church of Jesus Christ found in the Bible.

Satan has made it so hard to differentiate between true Christianity, denominationalism and Roman Catholicism. The majority of the world views Roman Catholics as "Christians." However, the Roman Catholic path to salvation is a stark contrast to what is taught in the Bible. This will be covered in the next chapter. Likewise, there are countless Protestant denominations that teach unscriptural methods to eternal life.

Another religion that falls under what is considered to be Christian is "Orthodox." Remember, Christianity was adopted by Constantine in 313 A.D. when he made the political resolution to combine church and state. Eventually, Constantine moved his headquarters to what is presently Istanbul, Turkey and there he formed the Eastern division of the Roman Empire. He named the headquarters, "Constantinople."

But, because the Church of Rome insisted on maintaining ultimate control over the entire temporal and spiritual world, a major schism occurred in 1054 A.D. between the Church of Rome in the West and the Orthodox Church in the East. The reason that this split occurred was because the Eastern Orthodox Church believed that the authority of the church needed to continue through "apostolic succession," but the Roman Catholic Church had built its authority on the papacy, an elected position. To this day, the Orthodox Church is under the authority of the patriarch, while the Roman Catholic Church is under the authority of the pope. In recent years, the schism has been mended and the Orthodox Church has joined hands in unity with the Roman Catholic Church in preparation for the future universal political and religious system under the Antichrist and his False Prophet.

In looking at the beliefs of the Orthodox Church, they are almost identical to that of Roman Catholicism, except that they do not accept the authority of the pope. The Orthodox Church believes[19]:

- That their church is "an ark" of salvation for anyone who wants to enter Heaven. They teach that this is the *only* true church established by Jesus Christ. In other words, there is no chance of being saved unless you are a member.
- The Nicene Creed.
- That Jesus is the Son of God.
- In the trinity.
- That Mary is the Mother of God and worshiped as such because she has "supreme grace" given to her by God.
- In the veneration of saints and intercedes to them before God.
- That the faith and doctrines of their Church can be found in the Holy Scriptures, the writings of the Church Fathers and the canons and decrees of the Seven Ecumenical Councils.
- That the Scriptures cannot be interpreted except by a priest.
- The real presence and divinity of Jesus in Holy Communion (transubstantiation- when the priest consecrates the bread

---

[19] http://serfes.org/orthodox/whatistheorthodoxchurch.htm

91

wafer, it magically changes into Jesus' *literal flesh* and the wine transforms into His *literal blood*.)
- In the veneration of special icons and relics of saints.
- That their seven sacraments are holy. They include: Baptism, Chrismation (Confirmation), Holy Eucharist (Holy Communion), Confession, Ordination, Marriage and Holy Unction. They teach that Baptism and Chrismation are the means of entrance into the Orthodox Church.

We have dealt with most of the counterparts of what is considered "Christianity" and the Roman Catholic Church will be covered in more detail in the next chapter. Now, we will move onto another of the monotheistic religions, Judaism.

JUDAISM

The religion of Judaism is the foundation of all of the religions previously mentioned. This was the religion of God's chosen people, the Jews. We have already given a great deal of information on how Judaism was birthed, through the lineage of Abraham, Isaac and Jacob. Judaism is the only major religion that was instituted from a particular bloodline.

We must differentiate that while Judaism is a religion, the Jews are an ethnic race. Not all Jews practice Judaism and not all that practice Judaism are Jews. This is because someone who is not a Jew by birth can convert to Judaism. Also, someone who is ethnically Jewish may have nothing to do with the traditions of the religion of Judaism. As a matter of fact, the percentages of non-religious or secular Jews living in the homeland of Israel is staggering, at about 42%.[20] There are three major sects of Judaism[21]:

- *Orthodox Judaism* is the oldest branch and they strictly adhere to the original form of Judaism's customs, practices and traditions. Every word of the Torah, or Old Testament, is considered to be divinely inspired and mandatory. Worship is in a synagogue, where only the Hebrew language is used.
- *Reform Judaism* is the more liberal side of Judaism which began in Germany in 1790. This sect follows the ethical laws of Judaism, but the traditional customs, such as strict diet and dress code, are largely ignored. They worship in a temple instead of a synagogue where English is permissible over the traditional Hebrew, and where musical instruments are allowed. Unlike Orthodox Judaism, there is no gender segregation and even females can be Rabbis. Instructions from God can be influenced by history and culture.
- *Conservative Judaism* hovers between the two mentioned above by retaining much of the traditions, but makes accommodations for contemporary lifestyles. Some dietary restrictions apply, but not all as in the Orthodox sect. Worship is in both Hebrew and English.

There are also some minor Jewish movements[22]:

---

[20] www.israelnationalnews.com/News/News.aspx/148286
[21] *World Religions and Cults 101*, Bickel and Jantz, Harvest House Publishers, 2002, page 49
[22] *World Religions and Cults 101*, Bickel and Jantz, Harvest House Publishers, 2002, page 50

- *Hasidic Judaism* emphasizes joy and emotion instead of intellectualism.
- *Humanistic Judaism* encompasses those Jews who are ethnically Jewish, but are mostly Agnostic or Atheist.
- *Reconstructionism* is a radical group who view Judaism as a civilization instead of a religion and claim that the Jews are not God's chosen people.
- *Zionism* seeks to colonize the Jews in the land of Israel after their diaspora, or dispersion. They have worked persistently to bring the Hebrew language back and to keep the Jews from losing their national identity because of the persecution and death of so many Jews over the centuries.

Judaism is not strict on doctrine and within their belief system, actions are more important than a particular statement of faith. One overriding doctrinal truth of Judaism is in *Shema*, which faithful Jews are to recite twice daily. Shema says, *"Hear, O Israel, The Lord is our God, the Lord is one."*

The widely accepted thirteen principles written by Rabbi Moses Maimonides (1135-1204 A.D.) are considered to be the basic tenets of Judaism.[23] These tenets are:

1. God exists and is the sole Creator.
2. There is only one, unique God.
3. God has no bodily shape or form.
4. God is eternal.
5. We should pray to God and to Him only.
6. The words of the prophets are true.

---

[23] *World Religions and Cults 101*, Bickel and Jantz, Harvest House Publishers, 2002, page 48

7. The prophecies of Moses are true, and he is the greatest of the prophets.
8. The written Torah (the five books of the Tanakh) and the Oral Torah (the teachings of the Talmud) are true.
9. The Torah is not subject to change, and there will never be another Torah from God.
10. God knows the thoughts and deeds of every person.
11. God will reward those who are good and will punish those who are wicked.
12. The Messiah will come.
13. The dead will be resurrected.

In the religion of Judaism, Jehovah God is seen as the powerful ruler of the Universe. He is a loving and just God and mankind is able to communicate with Him. They believe that man is basically good because he was created in the image of God. Man has the ability to make ethical choices and is responsible for his own actions. When it comes to the issue of sin, Judaism believes that man has a good nature, but evil may lead him astray.

The concept of salvation and an afterlife is not well developed in Judaism. Man's external existence is determined by his moral behavior and attitudes. They believe that God offers forgiveness to those who repent and atone for their sins through positive action. Further, they teach that man is responsible for leading a moral life while here on Earth and any judgment in the afterlife is left up to God's discretion.

Morality and the desired patterns for behavior are addressed in Jewish literature and based upon the good of the community, as well as, social justice. Judaism greatly values marriage and children. Worship is a major part of Jewish life, with rituals and ceremony playing an important role in their prayer-centered worship.

When it comes to the issue of Jesus, some recognize that He was a great teacher of morality, but most consider Him to be an imposter Messiah. Judaism does not believe that the Messiah has made His appearance, so they are still patiently awaiting His arrival. The Jews would still be performing the animal sacrifices if the second Jewish Temple had not been destroyed in 70 A.D. by the Roman General Titus. This was allowed by God because the sacrificial system was no longer needed after the final **"Lamb of God"** paid the sin debt once and for all.

It is interesting that the Early Christian Church, as recorded in the Book of Acts and in the Epistles, was initially made up of mostly Jews. But Peter, the apostle to the Jews, was encouraged in a vision given by God, to extend the Gospel to the Gentiles (Acts Chapter 11). Paul, the apostle to the Gentiles, was given the understanding of the New Covenant (Galatians 1: 12) and many Gentiles became Christians and joined the Early Church.

This is the same Christian Church today that true believers in Jesus Christ have joined, the Body of Christ, *His true Church.* These people believe in the finished work of Jesus on the Cross for their salvation and rely on no ecclesiastical structure or hierarchy to dictate God's design for mankind. Everything else we will review, as you will see, comes directly from philosophies created by fallen unredeemed man.

ISLAM

The last of the big three monotheistic religions we will dig into is Islam, which was created in the 7th century by Muhammad. This religion was birthed out of the Eastern division of the Roman Empire. The word "Islam" means *"submission,"* and the followers of Islam are called "Muslims." It is important to understand that Islam is more than a religion, it is also a way of life for Muslims.

Islam mimics the culture of 7th century Arabia, when Muhammad claimed to receive mystical visions from the angel Gabriel who told him that Allah was the one true God. In reality, Allah is the personal name used by pagans for the moon god, which they prayed to while facing Mecca, because the statue of Allah was located there.[24]

Muhammad created the religion of Islam and used brute force to gain converts. The followers of Islam are taught that they will enter "Paradise" upon death if they follow the rules and rituals set forth by Muhammad. "Paradise" is described as having all of the lusts of the flesh which are forbidden here on Earth.

Muhammad could neither read nor write, so after his death, his followers took many of his visions and put them on paper, thereby creating the Qur'an, the sacred book of Islam. Muslims are taught from birth to spread the words of the Qur'an by the sword, and to kill any "infidels," or unbelievers, who deny that Allah is the one true God. This is the cause for much of the bloodshed in the Middle East.

Islam has Five Pillars of Faith, which we will briefly cover.[25] The first is their creed, which is known in Arabic as *Shahada,* meaning "to bear witness." A Muslim must recite publically every day, *"There is no God but Allah, and Muhammad is his messenger."* Reciting this mantra publically professes a Muslim's membership in the Islamic faith.

The next pillar is Muslim prayer or *Salat,* which they believe shows obedience to Allah and must be performed five times

---

[24] http://www.biblebelievers.org.au/islam.htm
[25] http://www.religionfacts.com/five-pillars-islam

daily. These prayers must be said at dawn, noon, mid-afternoon, after sunset and at night, and they must always face Mecca in Saudi Arabia. Most of the time the prayers can be said at home or a workplace, but on Fridays, the Muslim must attend a mosque, an Islamic place of worship, at noon to pray.

The third pillar is the giving of alms, known in Arabic as *Zakat*. It comprises 2.5% of a Muslim's income and the money is used within the community for welfare and also used to build and maintain mosques.

Pillar number four is fasting or *Sawn*. For the whole month of *Ramadan*, Muslims abstain from food, drink and pleasures from sunrise to sunset each day during this month.

The final fifth pillar is pilgrimage, or *Hajj* in Arabic. Once in a Muslim's lifetime, each person is required to visit Mecca, the sacred city of Islam. The visit must take place during the last month of the Islamic year in order to fulfill the requirements of the Hajj.

The Five Pillars of Faith are used to gain love from Allah because Muslims believe that Allah is a god of judgment and power, not a god of love, grace and mercy. Islam teaches that each Muslim has two recording angels who weigh their good and bad deeds on a scale and play an important role on Judgment Day.

There are many sects of Islam, but the two more popular divisions are Sunni and Shi'ite. The Sunnis are the larger of the two, comprising about 80% of the Muslim population. They are known as "followers of the tradition," or "followers of the path." They believe that leaders of Islam should be elected and that there should be a separation of religion and politics.

Shi'ites, on the other hand, believe that the successor of Muhammad should only be someone in Muhammad's bloodline. They claim that the Islamic caliph, or religious leader, is also a government leader. Historically, the caliph was the political and religious leader of the entire Muslim community. It is interesting that, according to the Muslim *Hadith*, there are five stages of world history. The fifth and final stage begins with the return of the caliphate responsible for ushering in the Mahdi, the Islamic Messiah. The Islamic State, or ISIS, which has been in the news so much in the last few years, claims to be that very caliphate!

Here is a quick breakdown of the Islamic belief system.[26] As already stated, Muslims see Allah as the one true God and believe that he is the powerful ruler of the Universe. They deny the triune Godhead, comprised of God the Father, Jesus as the Son of God and the Holy Spirit. They see Allah as a judge and not as a loving god. The presence of Allah is not revealed through supernatural signs, but through the order of nature and the miracle of the Qur'an.

Islam teaches that humans are in charge of creation under the authority of Allah. Their charge is to instill moral order in the world through the teachings of Islam. When it comes to sin, they believe that each person is responsible for his evil deeds and these deeds are tracked throughout one's lifetime by the recording angels. They teach that the human inclination toward sin comes from weakness, rather than from the sin nature.

As far as salvation is concerned, Islam teaches that salvation is dependent upon a person's actions and attitudes during his lifetime. It is each person's own responsibility whether or not they will get to Paradise. They do not believe in having assurance of salvation or that you will know your eternal destiny until the Day of Judgment. This is when the scale will weigh your

---

[26] *World Religions and Cults 101*, Bickel and Jantz, Harvest House Publishers, 2002, page 76

good deeds against your bad deeds and determine whether you will enter Paradise or be tormented in Hell.

Islamic moral behavior is outlined in the teachings of the Qur'an and is seen in the acts of Muhammad, as recorded in the Hadith. For this reason, the Qur'an is perhaps the most memorized book in the world. A Muslim's true worship of Allah is best revealed by his strict adherence to the Five Pillars of Faith. Muslims don't think that they can communicate with Allah, so the prayers they offer and the works they do are the way that they worship Allah.

When it comes to the subject of Jesus, the Qur'an teaches that He was born of a virgin and led a sinless life. They believe that Jesus was a great prophet, but they do not believe that He was God. Muslims see Muhammad as the greatest prophet, so Jesus is a lesser prophet in their eyes.

Now that we have covered the beliefs of the big three monotheistic religions and investigated the historical beginnings of Judaism, Christianity, Roman Catholicism and Islam, it is time to elaborate on the beliefs of the Roman Catholic Church. She refers to herself as "Mother Church," and claims to have the keys to Heaven and Hell at her disposal.

Chapter Ten

THE MOTHER

The religion of Roman Catholicism is very near and dear to my own heart because I was baptized into this religion at only ten days old and spent thirty-two as a Roman Catholic. I attended thirteen years of Roman Catholic school and later, I was a teacher in a very prominent Roman Catholic school. But, the most interesting thing is that, despite all of those years of religion and attending Mass, I honestly knew nothing of my religion's beliefs. This is a pure case of "following the leader" and accepting that man could dictate to me how to reach God.

In 2005, after the Holy Spirit had persistently been dealing with me concerning my salvation, I finally said *"yes"* to becoming born again by accepting that I was a sinner and that Jesus paid my sin penalty on the Cross. I did not denounce my religion that very day, but it only took a short time for the Lord to show me that Roman Catholicism was a blatant contrast to the Christianity of the Bible. I discovered this by comparing *Roman Catholic Apologetics,* a book defending their belief system, to the information found in the Bible. There was no denying that the Church of Rome was full of canons, laws and sacraments, which were devised by man and enforced by an ecclesiastical structure.

As I dug deeper, the horrendous history of the Roman Catholic Church and their closet full of skeletons was revealed to me. I came to realize that this religion is Satan's *magnum opus,* his greatest work. It is Cain's altar, a new ornate cart and it is full of the pollution of idols, which are displayed in plain sight in their cathedrals. But, because it attaches the name "Christianity" to it,

Roman Catholics everywhere believe that they are "Christians." As a matter of fact, the *Catechism of the Catholic Church* states:

> All who have been justified by faith in Baptism are incorporated into Christ; they therefore have a right to be called Christians, and with good reason are accepted as brothers in the Lord by the children of the Catholic Church.[27]

In the last chapter, we touched on the historical beginnings of Roman Catholicism, which included the Roman Emperor Constantine's marriage of church and state in 313 A.D. This interlaced pagan emperor worship and Rome's Cult of Caesar with Christianity, as Constantine made it the state religion. His universal church eventually became known as the Roman Catholic Church and in 606 A.D., the Roman caesar took upon himself the title of "pope."[28]

Because Roman Catholicism is both a political and a spiritual institution, the popes began to claim universal temporal power and universal spiritual power over every person on the face of the whole Earth. The wealth and power that she obtained was staggering and because of persecution and the inquisitions, people were terrified to oppose her. They had every right to be afraid, because refusing to join meant death and many millions were martyred for their conflicting spiritual views. Much of this has been swept under the rug and the history books have been rewritten, so many do not realize the brutal past of the Roman Catholic Church.

---

[27] *Catechism of the Catholic Church,* 1994, paragraph 818, page 216
[28] *The Evangelist,* December 2006 edition, page 10

Why did I title this chapter "The Mother?" Other religions that we have covered claim the same exclusive means of salvation as the Roman Catholic Church does, but the Bible refers to her as **"THE MOTHER OF HARLOTS."** Revelation 17: 4-6 speaks of her saying, **"And the woman was arrayed in purple and scarlet colour, and decked with gold and precious stones and pearls, having a golden cup in her hand full of abominations and filthiness of her fornication. And upon her forehead was a name written, MYSTERY, BABYLON THE GREAT, THE MOTHER OF HARLOTS AND ABOMINATIONS OF THE EARTH. And I saw the woman drunken with the blood of the saints, and with the blood of the martyrs of Jesus..."**

Let's look at how this Scripture pertains to the Roman Catholic Church. First of all, the verses state that the woman is **"arrayed in purple and scarlet colour..."** Not only did the Roman emperor wear a purple robe, but these are also the colors worn by the Roman Catholic cardinals and bishops even today. The *Catholic Encyclopedia* describes the vestments of clergy where it says:

> The color for bishops and other prelates is purple, for the cardinals scarlet...[29]

The woman is also said to be **"decked with gold and precious stones and pearls,"** which obviously represents her tremendous wealth. The Roman Catholic Church has acquired great wealth over the centuries. This was mostly through forcible

---

[29] *Our Sunday Visitor's Catholic Encyclopedia,* Sunday Visitor Publishing Division, 1991, pg. 178

control and by selling salvation through the purchase of "indulgences." Indulgences promised to reduce time spent in Purgatory and the "temporal" punishment here on Earth. Many people believed that they were paying "installments" to get out of Purgatory quicker and into Heaven once they died. But, the money would continue to roll in after death because family members would pay indulgences for their deceased loved ones to be released from Purgatory sooner. Prior to the Reformation, a Dominican monk and "indulgence- vendor" named Johan Tetzel would say, *"As in the box the money rings the soul from Purgatory springs."*

Another large portion of the wealth came from the confiscated properties of "heretics," who would not accept the teachings of the Roman Catholic Church and were murdered during the many inquisitions. In the Spanish Inquisition alone, it is estimated that three million people were martyred by the Roman Catholic Church because they would not acknowledge the Church of Rome as the one true church.[30] It is difficult to imagine the money and land confiscated and added to the church treasury during this horrific period of history.

Also, since the Roman Catholic Church claimed to be the "one and only true church," kings were forced to donate land and money to avoid being excommunicated.[31] It is obvious that the great wealth of the Church of Rome has been acquired in very evil ways.

The passage in Revelation 17: 4 also states that the woman

_____

[30] *A Woman Rides the Beast,* Dave Hunt, Harvest House Publishers, Oregon, 1994, page 79
[31] *A Woman Rides the Beast,* Dave Hunt, Harvest House Publishers, Oregon, 1994, pages 83, 231

has **"a golden cup in her hand."** There is no coincidence that the Roman Catholic Church uses a golden chalice, an ornate gold cup, to pour the wine into during the celebration of the Eucharist. It is during this celebration that they believe the wafer of bread becomes Jesus' literal flesh and the wine becomes Jesus' literal blood. The *Catholic Encyclopedia* states:

> The chalice occupies the first place among sacred vessels, and by a figure of speech the material cup is often used as if it were synonymous with the precious blood itself.[32]

The Scripture states that this golden cup is **"full of abominations and filthiness of her fornication."** In 313 A.D., Jesus' true Church gave up hope of His return and signed a deal with the Devil when the Roman Emperor Constantine offered them freedom from persecution with his Edict of Milan. Many people abandoned true Christianity in an effort to build an earthly kingdom by "fornicating" with the political system of Rome.

The **"MOTHER OF HARLOTS"** also bears the name **"MYSTERY, BABYLON THE GREAT"** written on her forehead. The word "mystery" in **"MYSTERY, BABYLON THE GREAT"** separates spiritual Babylon from literal Babylon. The pagan roots of Roman Catholicism can be traced all of the way back to the Tower of Babel; the site which eventually became Babylon. It was here that Nimrod launched the construction of a tower in hopes of reaching Heaven (Genesis 11: 4). This was man's way of elevating himself to the level of God by his own efforts, which is identical to all forms of religion today.

---

[32] http://www.newadvent.org/cathen/03561a.htm

The Book of Revelation speaks of the Church of Pergamos. This Church is referred to as the state church or the "universal" Catholic Church under Constantine from about 300-500 A.D. Ironically, God refers to the Church of Pergamos as the seat of Satan. Revelation 2: 13, 14 says, **"I know your works, and where you dwell, even where Satan's seat is...where Satan dwells...who hold the doctrine of Balaam..."**

Now that we have reviewed the historical beginnings of Roman Catholicism and we have seen what the Book of Revelation reveals concerning her, let us look at what the Roman Catholic Church teaches and believes. While Roman Catholicism claims to acquire her beliefs from the Bible, you will find in a later chapter that she only views "sacred Scripture" as a portion of God's revelation to mankind.

The Roman Catholic Church is adamant that salvation can only be administered to her faithful members. The *Catechism of the Catholic Church* states:

> Basing itself on Scripture and Tradition, the Council teaches that the Church, a pilgrim now on earth, is necessary for salvation...Hence they could not be saved who, knowing that the Catholic Church was founded as necessary by God through Christ, would refuse either to enter it or to remain in it.[33]

> The Second Vatican Council's Decree on Ecumenism explains, 'For it is through Christ's Catholic Church alone, which is the universal help toward salvation, that the fullness of the means of salvation can be

---

[33] *Catechism of the Catholic Church,* Second Edition, 1997, paragraph 846

obtained.'[34]

Former Pope Benedict XVI reaffirmed the Roman Catholic Church's stance on salvation on July 10, 2007, when he stated that she is:

> The one and only true church and that Orthodox Churches are defective, as well as, that other Christian denominations are not true churches.[35]

Paul rebukes the above statements concerning eternal salvation, when he says in Romans: 10: 9-10, **"If you shall confess with your mouth the Lord Jesus, and shall believe in your heart that God has raised Him from the dead, you shall be saved. For with the heart man believes unto righteousness; and with the mouth, confession is made unto salvation."** Then, in Romans 10: 13, Paul states, **"For whosoever shall call upon the name of the Lord shall be saved."** This message is reiterated countless times in the Bible by not only Paul, but by the mouth of Jesus Christ (John 1: 2; John 3: 36; John 5: 24; John 6: 47; John 3: 16; John 3: 18; John 6: 40).

The Roman Catholic Church teaches that an individual's salvation is based upon their merits or works by participating in her sacraments. But, did you know that the word "sacrament" is not found one single time in the Bible? According to the teachings of the Roman Catholic Church, Baptism is the first sacrament for eternal salvation. The *Catechism of the Catholic Church* states:

---

[34] *Catechism of the Catholic Church,* Second Edition, 1997, paragraph 816
[35] http://www.msnbc.msn.com/id/19692094/

The Church affirms that for believers the sacraments of the New Covenant are necessary for salvation.[36]

Baptism is birth into the new life in Christ. In accordance with the Lord's will, it is necessary for salvation, as is the Church herself, which we enter by Baptism... By Baptism *all sins* are forgiven, original sin and all personal sins, as well as all punishment for sin. In those who have been reborn nothing remains that would impede their entry into the Kingdom of God, neither Adam's sin, nor personal sin, nor the consequences of sin, the gravest of which is separation from God.[37]

Here marks the beginning of the "process" of working for salvation within the confines of the Roman Catholic Church. The claim is that the Roman Catholic Church and baptism are necessary for salvation; even claiming that baptism washes away our sin. Let us look at 1 Peter 3: 2 1, where it states, **"The like figure whereunto even baptism does also now save us (not the putting away of the filth of the flesh, but the answer of a good conscience toward God,) by the Resurrection of Jesus Christ."**

Our water baptism does not wash away the **"filth of our flesh"** as the Roman Catholic Church claims. However, when we accept Jesus Christ as our Lord and Saviour, we are baptized *into* His death and raised to newness of life. There is a difference between water baptism and baptism into the death of Christ. Romans 6: 3-4 states, **"Know you not, that so many of us as were baptized into Jesus Christ were baptized into His Death?**

---

36 *Catechism of the Catholic Church,* 1994, paragraph 1129
37 *Catechism of the Catholic Church,* Second Edition, 1997, paragraph 1277

Therefore we are buried with Him by baptism into death: that like as Christ was raised up from the dead by the Glory of the Father, even so we also should walk in newness of life."

Water baptism is symbolic and should be a conscious decision by an individual to be identified with the death of Christ and to be raised up by God into a new life. Galatians 2: 20 says, **"I am Crucified with Christ: nevertheless I live; yet not I, but Christ lives in me: and the life which I now live in the flesh I live by the Faith of the Son of God, Who loved me, and gave Himself for me."** Most Roman Catholics are mere infants when they are baptized, which means there was no free will concerning their choice in the matter.

There are many more works, or sacraments, which are required by the Roman Catholic Church for salvation. The seven sacraments of the Roman Catholic Church are: Baptism, Confirmation, Eucharist, Penance, Anointing of the Sick, Holy Orders and Matrimony.[38] These sacraments claim to obtain certain "graces" for the faithful Catholic.[39]

In John 19: 30, Jesus cried out, **"It is finished,"** just moments before He freely gave up His life on the Cross. His death was a complete work and when we place our faith in His finished work, then we are instantaneously saved. In other words, the "graces" of the Roman Catholic sacraments are unnecessary because the work of salvation was *finished* at Calvary.

Even those devout Roman Catholics, who take part in all of the sacraments and rituals of this Church, are not promised to make it to Heaven upon death, because the Roman Catholic religion teaches the doctrine of "Purgatory." The idea of Purgatory

---

[38] http://www.newadvent.org/library/almanac_13295a.htm
[39] http://www.newadvent.org/cathen/13295a.htm

was established by Pope Gregory the Great in 593, but was not made doctrine until 1439 by the Council of Florence.[40] According to the Roman Catholic Church, Purgatory is an intermediate place where the soul is purified and made ready for Heaven.[41] Roman Catholicism declares:

> Sins must be expiated. This may be done on this earth through the sorrows, miseries and trials of this life and, above all, through death. Otherwise the expiation must be made in the next life through fire and torments or purifying punishments...[42]

There is no mention in the Bible of a place called Purgatory because Jesus purged our sins once and for all on the Cross. Hebrews 1: 3 says, **"Who being the brightness of His Glory, and the express image of His person, and upholding all things by the Word of His power, when He had by Himself purged our sins, sat down on the right hand of the Majesty on High."** The fact that Jesus **"sat down on the right hand"** of God signifies a finished and completed work. The Bible also says in Hebrews 9: 27, **"...it is appointed unto men *once* to die, but after this the Judgment** (My italics).**"**

How can a person be released from Purgatory according to the teachings of the Roman Catholic Church? The *Catechism of the Catholic Church* states that you can begin right here on Earth by paying for or participating in "indulgences," which claim to reduce your "temporal punishment" here on Earth and in

---

[40] *The Evangelist,* December 2006 edition, page 10
[41] *Catechism of the Catholic Church,* Second Edition, 1997, paragraph 1031, 1472
[42] Apostolic Constitution on the Revision of Indulgences, Vatican II

Purgatory. [43] You can also hope that once you die, your loved ones will pay for Roman Catholic Masses to be said in your name or will pray you into Heaven by reciting the Rosary to Mary. The *Catechism of the Catholic Church* states under the heading, *"What is an indulgence?"*

> An indulgence is a remission before God of the temporal punishment due to sins whose guilt has already been forgiven, which the faithful Christian who is duly disposed gains under certain prescribed conditions through the action of the Church which, as the minister of redemption, dispenses and applies with authority the treasury of the satisfactions of Christ and the Saints...An indulgence is partial or plenary according as it removes either part or all of the temporal punishment due to sin. The faithful can gain indulgences for themselves or apply them to the dead. [44]

If that statement sounds just like an insurance policy, it is because this is exactly what they are selling: *insurance for Heaven!* In 1 Peter 1: 18-19 it says, **"Forasmuch as you know that you were not redeemed with corruptible things, as silver and gold, from your vain conversation received by tradition from your fathers; But with the precious Blood of Christ, as of a Lamb without blemish and without spot..."** You cannot buy a ticket to Heaven because Jesus already purchased it with His sacrificial blood.

The Roman Catholic quotation concerning indulgences is

---

[43] *Catechism of the Catholic Church,* Second Edition, 1997, paragraph 1498
[44] *Catechism of the Catholic Church,* Second Edition, 1997, paragraph 1471

stating that faithful Roman Catholics can store up indulgences for themselves, thereby reducing their own time in Purgatory once they die; or they can obtain indulgences for someone who has already died in order to reduce the deceased person's time spent in Purgatory.

This is a massive money-making scheme! Did you know that St. Peter's Basilica in Rome was built with money from indulgence payments? In *History of the World,* by John C. Ridpath, it states:

> During the pontificate of Julius II, the completion and decoration of the new basilica of St. Peter's at Rome had been undertaken, and the sale of indulgences was relied upon to produce the necessary means for that great work.[45]

An example of an indulgence is that a person can receive three fewer years in Purgatory for making the "sign of the cross" and seven fewer years if it is made using "holy water," which is water sprinkled with salt and blessed by a priest.[46] Another example, which is given in *The Catholic Encyclopedia* as a way to be granted indulgences, is by devotion to Mary and the Rosary. It states:

> One of the many indulgences attached to the devotion [of Mary] is that the faithful who recite the Rosary together in a family group, besides the partial indulgence of ten years, are granted a plenary indulgence

---

[45] John C. Ridpath, *History of the World,* Volume IV, 1941, page 1601-1602
[46] *The Catholic Encyclopedia*, NY, Thomas Nelson Publishers, 1987, page 553

twice a month, if they perform this recitation daily for a month, go to Confession, receive Holy Communion, and visit some Church or public oratory.[47]

Sounds pretty complicated, doesn't it? It also mimics that "scale of salvation" where the good and bad deeds are weighed against one another. Remember the Scripture in 2 Corinthians 11: 3, where it states, **"But I fear, lest by any means, as the serpent beguiled Eve through his subtlety, so your minds should be corrupted from the simplicity that is in Christ."** Religious man tries to complicate the simple plan of salvation that God gave us in Jesus' death on the Cross. The truth is that if we could earn our way to Heaven, then there was no need for Jesus to come and die on the Cross.

Faithful Roman Catholics are not to commit the "sin of presumption," which means that no one can have any assurance of salvation. Through beautification and canonization, there is a process by which people are assumed to be in Heaven after death. The reigning pope is the only one who can say whether a person has become a "saint," and made it to Heaven. This process is very lengthy and requires tedious paperwork. Not even the pope of Rome is promised Heaven upon death!

There are degrees of sin in Roman Catholicism. *Venial sin* is considered less serious and *mortal sin* is much more serious. The Roman Catholic Church teaches that sin must be forgiven by a priest in the sacrament of Confession, because he is the only one who has the authority to absolve sin. The priest gives absolution and then a penance for the confessing sinner to complete. The *Catechism of the Catholic Church* states:

---

[47] *The Catholic Encyclopedia*, NY, Thomas Nelson Publishers, 1987, page 259

Indeed bishops and priests, by virtue of the sacrament of Holy Orders, have the power to forgive all sins 'in the name of the Father, and of the Son and of the Holy Spirit.'

Were there no forgiveness of sins in the Church, there would be no hope of life to come or eternal liberation. Let us thank God who has given his Church such a gift. [48]

Unfortunately, the Bible rebukes these statements in Mark 2: 7, where it states, **"Why does this man thus speak blasphemies? Who can forgive sins but God only?"** In the Old Testament, the Israelites did bring their sin offering to a priest, but the priesthood was abolished when Jesus died on the Cross and the Veil of the Temple was torn from top to bottom. Jesus gave us access to God and we no longer need another mediator between man and God than Jesus Christ. 1 Timothy 2: 5 explains, **"For there is one God, and one Mediator between God and men, the Man Christ Jesus..."**

The pope of the Roman Catholic Church is seen as the Vicar of Christ, or Christ's representative here on Earth, who dictates what God wants His people to know. Pope Leo XIII even said, *"We hold upon this earth the place of God Almighty."*[49] The *Catechism of the Catholic Church* states concerning the Roman Catholic pope:

---

[48] *Catechism of the Catholic Church*, 1994, paragraphs 1461, 983
[49] Pope Leo XIII, The Great Encyclical Letters of Leo XIII, Benzinger Brothers, New York, 1908, page 304

> For the Roman Pontiff, by reason of his office as Vicar of Christ, and pastor of the entire Church has full, supreme, and universal power over the whole Church, a power which he can always exercise unhindered.[50]

Roman Catholics believe that Peter was the first pope and that he was the head of the Church. Roman Catholics are taught that the pope is infallible, or without error, on subjects concerning doctrine, faith and morals. This became doctrine at the First Vatican Council in 1870. The *Catechism of the Catholic Church* states:

> The Roman Pontiff... enjoys this infallibility in virtue of his office, when as supreme pastor and teacher of all the faithful- who confirms his brethren in the faith-he proclaims by a definitive act a doctrine pertaining to faith or morals... This infallibility extends as far as the deposit of divine Revelation itself.[51]

To the Roman Catholic Church, infallibility means more than exemption from actual error; it means exemption from the *possibility* of error.[52] *The Catholic World* states:

> Each individual must receive the faith and law from the Church...with unquestioning submission and obedience of the intellect and will...We have no right to

---

[50] *Catechism of the Catholic Church*, 1994, paragraph 882
[51] *Catechism of the Catholic Church*, 1994, paragraph 891
[52] http://www.newadvent.org/cathen/07790a.htm

ask reasons of the Church, any more than of Almighty God...We are to take with unquestioning docility whatever instructions the Church give us.[53]

The Bible states concerning Jesus in Colossians 1: 18, **"And He is the head of the body, the Church: who is the beginning, the firstborn from the dead; that in all things He might have preeminence."** Then Ephesians 1: 22 says, **"And hath put all things under His feet, and gave Him to be the head over all things to the Church."**

The papacy and the hierarchy of cardinals, archbishops, bishops and priests are a foundation **"built upon the sand"** and not upon the Rock, Jesus Christ (Matthew 7: 26). Ephesian 5: 23 plainly states that **"Christ is the head of the Church."**

God did not send a mortal fallen man to guide and lead us, He sent the Holy Spirit to be our teacher, counselor and guide (John 14: 26; John 16: 1; 1 Corinthians 2: 11; 1 Corinthians 2: 12-13). When we yield our lives to God and are sensitive to the Holy Spirit, He will show us what is right and wrong.

"Transubstantiation" is the most important doctrine of the Roman Catholic Church. The doctrine of transubstantiation was decreed by Pope Innocent III in 1215 A.D.[54] This doctrine states that the wafer of bread and the wine are mysteriously transformed into the *literal* flesh and *literal* blood of Jesus Christ by the priest who consecrates the host.[55] "*Hostia*" in Latin means "victim." Roman Catholicism teaches that Jesus offers Himself as

---

[53] *A Woman Rides the Beast,* Dave Hunt, Harvest House Publishers, Oregon, 1994, page 88
[54] *The Evangelist,* December 2006 edition, page 11
[55] *Catechism of the Catholic Church,* Second Edition, 1997, paragraph 1376

a victim to the priest to be sacrificed for the remission of sin.

This "consecrated" host is worshiped as though it is truly Jesus Christ. The doctrine of transubstantiation is the core of the Sacrifice of the Mass, called the Eucharist.[56] Many Roman Catholics believe that if they do not partake of the Eucharist each week at Mass, then they are committing a mortal sin, which is punishable by eternity in Hell.

Jesus should not be sacrificed day after day on altar after altar as is done in the Roman Catholic Churches across the world. Our sin debt was paid in full through the sacrifice of Jesus *once and for all* at Calvary. Hebrews 10: 11 says, **"And every Priest stands daily ministering and offering oftentimes the same sacrifices, *which can never take away sins*** (My italics)**."** Hebrews 9: 24-26 says, **"For Christ is not entered into the Holy Places made with hands...but to Heaven itself, now to appear in the presence of God for us: Nor yet that He should offer Himself often, as the High Priest enters into the Holy Place every year with the blood of others** (speaking of the blood of the sacrificial animals, used to represent the blood which Jesus would shed for us)**; For then must He often have suffered since the foundation of the world: but now once in the end of the world has He appeared to put away sin by the sacrifice of Himself."** Then Hebrews 10: 10 says, **"... we are sanctified through the Offering of the Body of Jesus Christ *once for all*** (My italics)**." "Once for all"** means that the sacrifice does not need repeating.

Faithful Roman Catholics may argue that they are not "re-sacrificing" Jesus at their Mass, but according to the Roman Catholic Church, the Eucharist is an "unbloody sacrifice" for the

---

[56] *Catechism of the Catholic Church,* Second edition, 1997, paragraph 1330

remission of sins.[57] Let us look at Hebrews 9: 22 where it states, **"...and without the shedding of blood is no remission** (of sin)**..."** This means that if there is no blood shed, then the sacrifice cannot take away sins; so an "unbloody sacrifice," as used in the Roman Catholic sacrament of the Eucharist, would be completely useless.

The Council of Trent in 1562 stated that the sacrifice of Christ and the sacrifice of the Eucharist are one single sacrifice and are one in the same:

> The victim is one and the same: the same now offers through the ministry of priests, who then offered himself on the cross; only the manner of offering is different... And since in this divine sacrifice which is celebrated in the Mass, the same Christ who offered himself once in a bloody manner on the altar of the cross is contained and offered in an unbloody manner . . . this sacrifice is truly propitiatory.[58]

This means that at the Roman Catholic Mass, Jesus Christ offers Himself by the hands of a priest as a true and real sacrificial offering to gain favor with or appease (propitiate[59]) God. The officiating priest actually says:

> Pray, brethren, that our sacrifice may be acceptable to God, the Almighty Father.

---

[57] http://www.newadvent.org/cathen/10006a.htm
[58] http://www.usccb.org/catechism/text/pt2sect2chpt1art3.htm
[59] http://www.merriam-webster.com/dictionary/propitiate

The congregation responds by saying:

> May the Lord accept the sacrifice at your hands
> for the praise and glory of His name, for our good, and the
> good of all His Church.

This can only mean that this is a new sacrifice each and every time it is performed. Hebrews 6: 6 and says, **"If they should fall away, to renew them again unto repentance; seeing they crucify to themselves the Son of God afresh, and put Him to an open shame."** Most Roman Catholics do not realize that the Sacrifice of the Mass is *repeating* the crucifixion of Jesus and thereby putting **"Him to an open shame."**

Other doctrines that set Roman Catholicism apart from true Christianity are the Marian Doctrines. The Roman Catholic Church esteems Mary, the mother of Jesus, very highly, even going so far as to claim that she is the source of salvation. The *Catechism of the Catholic Church* states:

> Mary is the symbol and the most perfect realization of the Church.[60]

> Being obedient she (Mary) became the cause of salvation for herself and for the whole human race.[61]

> Taken up to heaven she (Mary) did not lay aside this saving office but by her manifold intercession

---

[60] *Catechism of the Catholic Church,* Second Edition, 1997, paragraph 507
[61] *Catechism of the Catholic Church,* 1994, paragraph 494, page 125

continues to bring us the gifts of eternal salvation.[62]

Down through the centuries, Roman Catholic popes have created their own doctrines concerning Mary. All of these doctrines elevate Mary to superhuman status and take the focus off of the real Redeemer, Jesus Christ. We will touch on each one briefly. First, we must deal with the fact that Mary is seen as a "mediator" between mankind and Jesus, and is even called a "*Mediatrix*" in the *Catechism of the Catholic Church*.[63] It also states:

> She (Mary) is inseparably linked with the saving work of her Son.[64]

The claim is that whatever we ask of Mary, she will plead for our requests at the feet of Jesus. However, remember that the Scripture plainly states in 1 Timothy 2: 5, **"For there is one God, and one Mediator between God and men, the Man Christ Jesus..."**

The first Marian doctrine to address is the *"Mary, the Mother of God"* doctrine. This was adopted by the Council of Ephesus in 431 A.D. and was reaffirmed by Pope Pius XI in 1931.[65] The *Catechism of the Catholic Church* states:

> Because she gives us Jesus, her son, Mary is Mother of God and our mother; we can entrust all our cares and petitions to her...By entrusting ourselves to her

---

[62] *Catechism of the Catholic Church,* 1994, paragraph 969, page 252

[63] *Catechism of the Catholic Church,* Second Edition, 1997, paragraph 969, 2674

[64] *Catechism of the Catholic Church,* 1994, paragraph 1172. page 303

[65] *The Evangelist,* December 2006 edition, page 12

prayer, we abandon ourselves to the will of God together with her.[66]

The Bible states that the Godhead consists of God the Father; Jesus, the Living Word of God, as well as, the Incarnate Son of God; and the Holy Spirit. God is **"the Alpha and the Omega, the beginning and the end"** (Revelation 21: 6), so for the Roman Catholic Church to claim that Mary is the "Mother of God" is incorrect. Mary did not give birth to God, but to the incarnate physical body of the Son of God, Jesus.

The Bible says that Jesus was **"...verily foreordained before the foundation of the world..."** (1 Peter 1: 20). This means that God knew man would fall and that He would send us a Redeemer, which was Jesus Christ.

The next Marian doctrine is *"Mary's bodily assumption into Heaven."* This doctrine was defined by Pope Pius XII in 1950.[67] The *Catechism of the Catholic Church* states:

> Finally the Immaculate Virgin, preserved free from all stain of original sin, when the course of her earthly life was finished, was taken up body and soul into heavenly glory, and exalted by the Lord as Queen over all things.[68]

God records the bodily assumption of Enoch and Elijah in the Bible, but not Mary? Why? Because, there is absolutely no Scriptural proof that Mary did not die an earthly death and instead was assumed into Heaven.

---

[66] *Catechism of the Catholic Church,* Second Edition, 1997, paragraph 2677
[67] http://www.catholicculture.org/library/view.cfm?recnum=469
[68] *Catechism of the Catholic Church,* Second Edition, 1997, paragraph 966

In another Marian doctrine, the Roman Catholic Church teaches that Mary is the *"Queen of Heaven."* This doctrine was officially declared in 1954 by Pope Pius XII.[69] The "Queen of Heaven" goes back all of the way to the Tower of Babel where paganism actually began.

This title can be found in the Bible, however, it refers to pagan gods. Jeremiah 7: 18 says, **"The children gather wood, and the fathers kindle fire, and the women knead their dough, to make cakes to the queen of heaven, and to pour out drink offerings unto other gods, that they may provoke Me** (God) **to anger."**

The next doctrine of the *"Immaculate Conception of Mary"* was established in 1854 A.D. by Pope Pius IX.[70] The meaning of this doctrine is that Mary was preserved free from original sin or the sin nature from the moment of her conception. The *Catechism of the Catholic Church* says:

> Through the centuries the Church has become ever more aware that Mary, 'full of grace' through God, was redeemed from the moment of her conception.[71]

The Bible says nothing about Mary being free from sin, but Romans 5: 12 does tell us that **"...by one man sin entered into the world, and death by sin; and so death passed upon all men, for that all have sinned."** There are Scriptures in Psalms 14: 3 and in Romans 3: 10 which say, **"There is none righteous, no, not one..."** Then a few verses later in Romans 3: 23 it says, **"For**

[69] http://www.newadvent.org/library/docs_pi12ac.htm
[70] *Catechism of the Catholic Church,* Second Edition, 1997, paragraph 491
[71] *Catechism of the Catholic Church,* Second Edition, 1997, paragraph 491

all have sinned, and come short of the Glory of God." Even Mary admits that she is in need of a Saviour in Luke 1: 46-47 where it says, **"And Mary said, My soul doth magnify the Lord, And my spirit has rejoiced in God my Saviour."**

The last of the Marian doctrines is Mary as *"the Most Blessed Virgin Mary,"* because it is believed that Mary was a perpetual virgin. This was made official by the Lateran Council in 649 A.D.[72] The *Catechism of the Catholic Church* states:

> Mary remained a virgin in conceiving her Son, a virgin in giving birth to him, a virgin in carrying him, a virgin in nursing him at her breast, always a virgin.[73]

While it is true that Mary conceived Jesus as a virgin under the power of the Holy Spirit (Luke 1: 35; Matthew 1: 18), there is no further proof or mention in the Bible of Mary living as a virgin for the rest of her life.

When the incarnate Jesus was placed in Mary's womb, she was engaged to Joseph (Luke 1: 27; Matthew 1: 18). They were married shortly thereafter and the Bible says in Matthew 1: 25, speaking of Joseph, **"And he knew her not till she had brought forth her First-born Son: and he called His name JESUS."** This verse reaffirms that Mary was a virgin at the time of Jesus' birth, but it says that Joseph **"knew her not *till* she had brought forth her First-born son (My italics)."** This does not mean that they *never* consummated their relationship, but means that it was not *until after* the birth of Jesus. Also, the Scripture says **"*her* First-born Son (My italics),"** referring to Mary having more than one

---

[72] http://www.catholic.org/featured/headline.php?ID=611
[73] *Catechism of the Catholic Church,* Second Edition, 1997, paragraph 510

son. Why would the Scripture say this if there were no other sons born to Mary following the birth of Jesus?

There is also proof that Jesus had legitimate siblings. In Matthew 13: 55-56, after Jesus teaches in the synagogue and the people are astonished by His wisdom, someone asks, **"Is not this the carpenter's son? Is not his mother called Mary? And His brethren, James, and Joses, and Simon, and Judas? And His sisters, are they not all with us?"**

If the Marian Doctrines were not enough to elevate Mary to the place of God, praying the Rosary to Mary is practiced by Roman Catholics all over the world. Among other things, it is believed that the recitation of the Rosary to Mary will reduce a loved one's time of burning in the "purging fires" of Purgatory. *The Catholic Encyclopedia* states concerning the origin of the Rosary that:

> ...when the Albigensian heresy (12th and 13th centuries) was devastating the country of Toulouse, St. Dominic earnestly besought the help of Our Lady (Mary) and was instructed by her, so tradition asserts, to preach the Rosary among the people as an antidote to heresy and sin.[74]

The use of prayer beads and repetitious prayer is also used in Buddhism, Hinduism and Islam. The Bible states in Matthew 6: 7, **"But when you pray, use not vain repetitions, as the heathen do: for they think that they shall be heard for their much speaking..."**

Roman Catholics are encouraged to pray to dead "saints."

---

[74] http://www.newadvent.org/cathen/13184b.htm

Saints are people who are presumed to be in Heaven and can intercede for the faithful Roman Catholic. *The Catechism of the Catholic Church* even goes so far as to state:

> Exactly as Christian communion (the Eucharist) among our fellow pilgrims brings us closer to Christ, so our communion with the saints joins us to Christ...[75]

In the Bible, the *living* believers in Jesus Christ are referred to as "saints" countless times. And as previously stated multiple times, there is only one mediator between God and man, Jesus Christ (1 Timothy 2: 5).

We already briefly touched on the fact that Roman Catholics believe that they can pray for their loved ones after death in order to release them from the purging fires of Purgatory. The *Catechism of the Catholic Church* states concerning this practice:

> In full consciousness of this communication of the whole Mystical Body of Jesus Christ, the Church in its pilgrim members, from the earliest days of the Christian religion, has honored with great respect the memory of the dead; and because it is a holy and wholesome thought to pray for the dead that they may be loosed from their sins she offers her suffrages for them. Our prayer for them is capable not only of helping them, but also making their intercession for us effective.[76]

The Roman Catholic Church also forbids their priests and

---

[75] *Catechism of the Catholic Church,* 1994, paragraph 957, pages 249-250
[76] *Catechism of the Catholic Church*, 1994, paragraph 958, page 250

nuns to marry. The *Catechism of the Catholic Church* states:

> All the ordained ministers of the Latin Church, with the exception of permanent deacons, are normally chosen from among men of faith who live a celibate life and who intend to remain celibate 'for the sake of the kingdom of heaven'... Celibacy is a sign of this new life to the service of which the Church's minister is consecrated; accepted with a joyous heart celibacy radiantly proclaims the Reign of God.[77]

Peter, the so-called first pope of Rome, was a married man, which is proven in Mark 1: 30. The Bible states first in Genesis 2: 18, **"...the LORD God said, It is not good than man should be alone, I will make him a help meet for him."** In Hebrews 13: 4, it says that **"Marriage is honorable in all."** 1 Timothy 3: 2 states, **"A bishop then must be blameless, the husband of one wife."**

But the Scripture that makes the most impact is found in 1 Timothy 4: 1-3, where it says, **"Now the spirit speaks expressly, that in the latter times some shall depart from the faith, giving heed to seducing spirits and doctrines of devils; speaking lies in hypocrisy; having their conscience seared with a hot iron; forbidding to marry, and commanding to abstain from meats; which God has created to be received with thanksgiving of them which believe and know the truth."**

Did you know that Vatican City, Rome, where the pope of Rome resides, is its very own sovereign state? This was signed

---

[77] *Catechism of the Catholic Church*, 1994, paragraph 1579, page 395

into action by Benito Mussolini in 1929 with the Lateran Pacts. Vatican City is the smallest country in the world at just over one hundred acres, making it just one eighth the size of Central Park in New York City. The Vatican mints its own euros, prints its own stamps, issues passports and license plates, operates media outlets, and has its own flag, anthem and police force.[78]

Roman Catholicism is much more than just a religion. It was formed out of the Roman Empire as a political and spiritual force which wants to control the whole world with its universal temporal and universal spiritual powers.

I have spent so much time on this chapter because Roman Catholicism is a large and very prominent religion, with over 1.2 billion adherents. Because Roman Catholicism is a political empire, as well as, a religious one, she plays a huge part in end time eschatology. Her doctrines, as anyone can see, are created by mortal man and also by twisting the Scriptures to justify some of her beliefs. The Early Church, under the disciples and apostles, was nothing like the elaborate religion which has been created by the hierarchy of the Roman Catholic Church.

In the Book of Revelation, we are presented with the Church of Thyatira, which historically became the papal church. The Church of Thyatira signifies the beginnings of organized Roman Catholicism, which began around 500 A.D. until present day. "Thyatira" comes from the two words meaning "sacrifice" and "continual." The bottom line is that the Roman Catholic Church denies the finished work of Christ and believes in a continual sacrifice of the Eucharist, which is performed at each and every celebration of the Mass. This is the most damnable heresy because

---

[78] http://www.google.com/amp/amp.hostory.com/news/10-things-you-may-not-know-about-the-vatican

denying the finished work of Christ is negating His once and for all sacrifice.

Let us end this chapter with Mark 7: 7, 8 and 13, where Jesus says, **"Howbeit in vain do they worship Me, teaching doctrines and commandments of men. For laying aside the commandments of God, you hold the tradition of men... Making the Word of God of none effect by your traditions."** Remember that Jesus is the "Word of God" made flesh to dwell among us and redeem us. The Church of Rome makes Jesus' sacrifice of none effect by their man-made traditions.

Chapter Eleven

WOULD YOU LIKE TO JOIN OUR CULT?

When we hear the word, "cult," many of us think of the phrase, *"Don't drink the Kool-Aid,"* but not all cults are like that of Jim Jones or David Koresh. A cult is a group of people, large or small, who have been indoctrinated to follow their leader without question. Most cults today have taken a system of beliefs and put their own twist on it so that it reaches way beyond its origins. Here are some earmarks of cults according to theologians Dr. R.C. Sproul and Tim Couch:[79]

- *An abrupt break with historic Christianity:* Cults usually view historical Christianity as being off base for the centuries since Christ until their founder came along.
- *Autosotericism:* This means "self-salvation," and most cults attempt to obtain salvation by following certain rules and regulations specified by the cult leader.
- *A deficient Christology:* Cults take a lesser view of Christ. They do not see Him as God or the Redeemer of mankind.

---

[79] *World Religions and Cults 101,* Bruce Bickel and Stan Jantz, Harvest House Publishers, 2002, pages 84-86

- *Syncretism:* Cults blend several different belief systems together into one.
- *Perfectionism:* Most cults teach that it is possible for humans to become morally perfect, or gods, by following the cults prescribed conduct codes.
- *An extra biblical source of authority:* Cults have their own holy books. Even if they claim to use the Bible, their own holy books take precedence over the Scriptures.
- *A belief in exclusive community salvation:* A cult teaches that it is the only true church and unless you believe in their teachings, you cannot be saved.
- *A preoccupation with eschatology:* Eschatology is the study of end times. Most cults will tell you that their founder has brought the last urgent word from God before the imminent end of the world.
- *Esotericism:* When something is esoteric, it is beyond the understanding of most people and only understood by a select few. Each cult claims that its founder or leader have access to special truths that were previously concealed.

The three cults that we will investigate in this chapter include Mormonism, Jehovah's Witnesses and Scientology. These religions are considered cults because they fit within the confines of the earmarks listed. Each of these three have multiple millions of followers, so it is important to know what they believe and how it contradicts with what we have already established as the truth found in God's Word. Much of the research information in this chapter was derived from *World Religions and Cults 101* by Bruce Bickel and Stan Jantz.

MORMONISM

Mormonism, or the Church of Jesus Christ of Latter Day Saints (LDS), was founded by Joseph Smith in 1830. It has grown from its original six members to well over 15 million devotees in over 30,000 congregations worldwide[80] It is one of the fastest growing cults with over 300,000 new converts each year.[81]

Mormons consider themselves to be Christians and will tell you that they believe in God, the Bible and Jesus Christ, but their actual beliefs tell a completely different story. Their founder, Joseph Smith, claims to have received a vision in 1820, when God and Jesus appeared and told him that all of the current churches were wrong in their beliefs. He was told that a new church was to be founded and that he was appointed to be the leader.

Later, in 1823, Joseph Smith requested another vision and that is when he says the angel Moroni appeared and told him that a book inscribed on gold plates was buried somewhere near his home. The book was said to have an account of the true gospel given to the ancient inhabitants of the land by the "Savior." Three years later, when the angel Moroni finally told Joseph Smith of the location, he claims to have dug up the gold plates. He then transcribed the reformed Egyptian hieroglyphics using his seer stone, known as the "urim and the thumin," which was found buried with the plates.

Smith published the translation of the gold plates in 1830 and called it the *Book of Mormon*. He also founded the Mormon

---

[80] https://www.mormonnewsroom.org/facts-and-statistics/
[81] *World Religions and Cults 101,* Bruce Bickel and Stan Jantz, Harvest House Publishers, 2002, page 91

Church at the same time and began gaining converts in Ohio, Missouri and Illinois. As the Mormon Church grew, so did the opposition to Joseph Smith's unorthodox views. He continued to receive "revelations" concerning topics of the Godhead, the origin and destiny of the human race, eternal progression, baptism of the dead and polygamy.

The practice of polygamy, or having multiple wives, is what caused the most objections. Would you believe that Joseph Smith had thirty wives of his very own? In June of 1844, when Joseph Smith was imprisoned for rioting and charged with treason and conspiracy, a mob of 200 stormed the jail and killed him.

His successor, Brigham Young, led the Mormons to Salt Lake City, Utah and established "the new Zion." Mormons continued in polygamy until 1890, when Wilford Woodruff had a new revelation that Mormons were to give up this practice. Ironically, this "new revelation" came at the same time that the United States government had threatened to confiscate the Mormon Church's temple and deny Utah the opportunity for statehood if the practice of polygamy persisted.

Let's look at some of the beliefs of the Mormon Church. First of all, what do they teach about the nature of God? In Mormonism, God is not the omniscient, omnipotent, omnipresent deity described in the Bible. Instead, they believe that God was once mortal man who progressed over time to become God. Mormon theologian, Milton R. Hunter stated:

God the Eternal Father was once a mortal man who passed through a school of earth life similar to that through which we are now passing. He became God-an exalted being- through obedience to the same eternal

Gospel truths that we are given the opportunity to obey today.[82]

With that said, Mormons believe that they too can achieve the same state of godhood. Therefore, Mormons practice polytheism, the belief in multiple gods. They believe in the eternal progression of other gods and that the present "Father God" descended from other gods before Him. Specifically, according to Mormon theology, the current Father God was created, grew up as a man on another planet and then became God. He procreated with the Mother God and had millions of spirit children.

The firstborn of these spirit children was Jesus and the second was Lucifer. That's right, according to the Mormon Church, Jesus and Lucifer are brothers! Does the Bible say anything of this nature? Absolutely not! Lucifer is an angel, and angels are a completely different race than humans. How, then, can Jesus and Lucifer be flesh and blood brothers?

What about the other millions of spirit children? Mormons believe that God's plan for them was to populate Earth, be tested and then to return to Him upon death. They teach that Lucifer was angry that Jesus was chosen to be the Saviour, so he rebelled against God and was banished from Heaven to Earth.

According to the teachings of the Mormon Church, Jesus was born on Earth by God having intercourse with Mary. They believe that Jesus grew up, got married and had children of His own. Some even believe that Jesus was a polygamist. They do teach that Jesus died on the Cross, was resurrected with a new body and

---

[82] *World Religions and Cults 101,* Bruce Bickel and Stan Jantz, Harvest House Publishers, 2002, page 98

returned to Heaven, where He is waiting to takes the place of Father God once God progresses to an even higher realm.

Mormons believe in preexistence, where they teach that every person once existed as a spirit in Heaven. You can progress toward godhood by becoming a Mormon, following their rules and getting married in a Mormon temple. Those who do this will receive their very own planet, and then once they become gods, they will have their own spirit children. These spirit children will eventually come to Earth and repeat the same cycle.

As far as sin and salvation are concerned, Mormons teach that each person is born innocent. They do not teach that sin is rebellion against God, but is instead simply making a mistake. Salvation to a Mormon is that he or she will be resurrected and have a body. The process of salvation is dependent on good works and obeying the "gospel" of the Mormon Church.

Mormonism claims that all people are eventually saved, but when a Mormon dies, he will enter one of three heavens ranging from the best to the not so good: celestial, terrestrial, or telestial. Only Mormons who have faithfully followed the teachings of the Mormon Church will enter the celestial. There is no mention of Hell in Mormon teachings.

Almost every doctrine of the Mormon Church is contrary to the Scriptures found in the Bible. Their teachings were created from the mind of mortal men. God's Word does not contradict itself and Jesus Christ is **the same yesterday, today and forever** (Hebrews 13: 8)." The "revelations" that the founder of the Mormon Church claims to have experienced, were not from God. The fact that almost 15 million people subscribe to these strange and unscriptural doctrines is both alarming and sad. So, despite the fact that most Mormons appear to be morally upright, their righteousness is based on following a man-made religious cult.

JEHOVAH'S WITNESSES

The next religious cult we will investigate is Jehovah's Witnesses. They are highly organized and work very hard to gain converts. Most of us have heard that polite knock on our doors and have had encounters with Jehovah's Witnesses. They will proudly identify themselves as "Christians," but just as with Mormons, their teachings are contrary to the Bible in many ways.

Before we dive into the beliefs of Jehovah's Witnesses, let us look at the origins of this religion. This movement began in 1872 by Charles Taze Russell in Pittsburgh, Pennsylvania. Russell was raised in traditional Christianity, but as a young man, he became skeptical about the existence of Hell and later became intrigued about the imminent return of Jesus Christ to establish the Millennial Kingdom. He predicted that this would take place in 1914 and went on to print *The Watchtower* magazine.

When 1914 came and went and Jesus did not return, Charles T. Russell made other predictions, but none of them ever came to pass. He died in 1916 and was succeeded by Joseph Rutherford. Rutherford's writings became the new standard for doctrinal reinterpretation, even though they contradicted Charles T. Russell's many writings. He introduced another magazine, now known as *Awake*, and reinforced the door-to-door witnessing. The name "Jehovah's Witnesses" became official in 1931.

Upon the death of Joseph Rutherford, Nathan H. Knorr became the president. During his presidency, the Jehovah's Witnesses grew exponentially following his establishment of special training schools for missionaries worldwide.

The number of Jehovah's Witnesses today is difficult to calculate. Those who log their hours of witnessing door-to-door are considered "publishers," and that number is over 8 million. However, at the annual Memorial Service, there were over 20 million in attendance.[83] This number is even larger than that of the Mormon Church!

Now, let us look at the beliefs and teachings of Jehovah's Witnesses. They will openly tell you that the Bible is their only authority, but they use their own version of the Bible called the New World Translation. They believe that it can only be interpreted by a Jehovah's Witness. They believe in God, but not in the Godhead, which consists of God the Father, Jesus Christ and the Holy Spirit as one God manifested in three persons. According to the Jehovah's Witnesses, the correct name for God is "Jehovah."

Jehovah's Witnesses do not believe that Jesus is the Son of God or that He is deity at all. They teach that Jesus is actually the archangel Michael, the first of God's creations, who was called "Jesus" when He came to Earth. Once Jesus was resurrected and returned to Heaven, He was again known as "Michael." No one is allowed to pray to Jesus, because He is not God. The Holy Spirit is seen as an active force, like electricity.

Jehovah's Witnesses believe that the afterlife is only for their members, and like Charles T. Russell, they do not believe in eternal punishment in Hell. All of the non-Jehovah's Witnesses are simply evaporated after death, with no afterlife of any kind.

While they teach that every Jehovah's Witness will have an afterlife, they only believe that 144,000 will actually go to Heaven. The others will live on a regenerated Earth for eternity, once Jehovah establishes the Millennial Kingdom. Until that time, any Jehovah's Witness who dies will remain in "soul sleep," or unconsciousness until they are resurrected in the Millennium.

---

[83] http://www.jwfacts.com/watchtower/statistics.php

Jehovah's Witnesses believe in salvation, but it must be earned. Salvation does not come from Jesus' death on the Cross, because Jesus is not seen as deity. They believe Jesus died on a stake and was cursed by God. They count on their works as witnesses and testifying for Jehovah to be the source of their salvation. Jehovah's Witnesses believe that sin is simply falling short of God's perfection. They teach that sin was passed down from Adam and Eve and that Jesus' death on the Cross canceled out Adam's sin and brought back the possibility of the perfection of man.

There is a strict governing body for Jehovah's Witnesses located in Brooklyn, New York, where doctrine is dictated to the Witnesses worldwide. Jehovah's Witnesses must meet their weekly and monthly requirements where they are to study *The Watchtower* magazine and other Watchtower publications at their local "Kingdom Hall." There is no active participation in these meetings, as there are no questions allowed. The teachings of the Watchtower Society are to be accepted as authoritative, definitive and final.

True "worship" of a Jehovah's Witness comes in the form of adhering to the many requirements, such as the five hours of weekly meetings, witnessing door-to-door, abstaining from parties, holidays, celebrations, displays of patriotism, military service and blood transfusions.

It is interesting that Jehovah's Witnesses will assume the title of "Christians," when they deny foundational Christian beliefs such as the Godhead, the deity of Jesus Christ and salvation through Jesus' death on the Cross. They are informed on exactly what to say and also instructed to take no materials from their potential converts. They are coached by man and not sent by God. Jehovah's Witnesses beliefs do not resemble Christianity at all, yet they flock to neighborhood after neighborhood knocking on doors and attempting to persuade others to join their warped "Christian" cult.

SCIENTOLOGY

To better understand the next religious cult, it is best to take a look at the beliefs posted on their official Scientology website. This explanation is given under the title, *"What is Scientology?"*[84]

> Developed by L. Ron Hubbard, Scientology is a religion that offers a precise path leading to a complete and certain understanding of one's true spiritual nature and one's relationship to self, family, groups, mankind, all life forms, the material universe, the spiritual universe and the Supreme Being.
>
> Scientology addresses the spirit – not the body or mind – and believes that man is far more than a product of his environment or his genes.
>
> Scientology comprises a body of knowledge which extends from certain fundamental truths. Prime among these are: Man is an immortal spiritual being; His experience extends well beyond a single lifetime; His capabilities are unlimited, even if not presently realized.
>
> Scientology further holds man to be basically good, and that his spiritual salvation depends on himself, his fellows and his attainment of brotherhood with the Universe.
>
> Scientology is not a dogmatic religion in which one is asked to accept anything on faith alone. On the contrary, one discovers for himself that the principles of

---

[84] https://www.scientology.org/what-is-scientology.html

Scientology are true by applying its principles and observing or experiencing the results.

The ultimate goal of Scientology is true spiritual enlightenment and freedom for all.

The founder of Scientology, L. Ron Hubbard was influenced by his travels and life experiences. After working as a sea captain in World War II and watching the soldiers struggle to recover from mental, as well as, physical injuries, Hubbard set out to discover what became known as Dianetics. He published a book by the same name in 1950, *Dianetics: The Modern Science of Mental Health.* The book quickly became a New York Times best seller and stayed on the list for twenty-six consecutive weeks. Scientology was born as a result of the interest in L. Ron Hubbard's work. He bridged the gap between East and West and between science and religion.[85]

Hubbard's works on Dianetics and Scientology comprise more than 5,000 writings and 3,000 recorded lectures, where he claims to have the answers to the most profound mysteries of life, death and the afterlife. Also, his works aim to aid in raising children, repairing families, educating, organizing and providing relief in times of illness or suffering.[86] Hubbard claimed that through Dianetics, one could be cured of psychosomatic disorders.

A fundamental principle of Scientology is the view of man as a spiritual being, who simply occupies a body. This is called a *thetan*, because the term is taken from the Greek letter *theta* for "thought," "life" or "the spirit." The thetan is thought to be immortal and has lived and will continue to live through multiple

---

[85] https://www.scientology.org/l-ron-hubbard/
[86] https://www.scientology.org/l-ron-hubbard/

and countless lifetimes. The thetan animates the body and uses the mind.

Also essential to Scientology is the view of life as compartmentalized into certain impulses toward survival. These are called the *dynamics* and there are Eight Dynamics ranging from the drive toward self-existence to the final dynamic of urge toward existence as infinity or Supreme Being.[87]

Through the process of "auditing," a Scientologist can travel to higher states of spiritual awareness. This can be accomplished one of two ways: By helping individuals rid themselves of any spiritual disabilities and by increasing spiritual abilities through the Eight Dynamics. The goal of auditing is to "restore beingness and ability".[88] There are trained ministers within Scientology, called auditors, who help with the process.

Ultimately, Scientologists view life as "a game," which everyone has a chance to win.[89] The goal of life is considered to be infinite survival. On the contrary, pain, disappointment and failure are the results of actions that hinder infinite survival. Of course, this is all dependent on the individual's own actions and reactions. There is no dependence on God or Jesus.

The Scientology website concludes concerning the concept of God:

> Only when the Seventh Dynamic (spiritual) is
> reached in its entirety will one discover and come to a full

---

[87] https://www.scientology.org/faq/background-and-basic-principles/what-are-some-of-the-core-tenets-of-scientology.html

[88] https://www.scientology.org/faq/scientology-and-dianetics-auditing/what-is-auditing.html

[89] https://www.scientology.org/faq/scientology-attitudes-and-practices/how-do-scientologists-view-life.html

understanding of the Eighth Dynamic (infinity) and one's relationship to the Supreme Being.[90]

While L. Ron Hubbard was a well-traveled, intelligent man, his beliefs and conclusions about mankind come from within his own mind. Although, Hubbard died in 1986, Scientology claims to continue to gain converts. As far as the population of Scientology, that is difficult to number. They have 11,000 churches worldwide, but no one seems to be able to give a viable number of members. Some say only 30,000-50,000, while the current leader, David Miscavige, has claimed that Scientology has 10 million members. Regardless, this religious cult deserved at least a few pages of attention and has again been proven to be contrary to God's plan of salvation given in the Bible.

There are many more cults looking for members to brainwash with their man-made doctrines and beliefs. Personally, I find the beliefs of Mormons, Jehovah's Witnesses and Scientologists to be bizarre and dangerous, but likely, I could easily be fooled if I did not have true Christianity and God's plan of salvation to make comparisons. If we are not grounded in the truth found in God's Word, then it is so easy to be deceived and blinded by the unscriptural promises made by these cults.

---

[90] https://www.scientology.org/faq/scientology-beliefs/what-is-the-concept-of-god-in-scientology.html

Chapter Twelve

DHARMA, KARMA, NIRVANA & CONFU-SION

The philosophical religions covered in this chapter all originated in the Eastern part of the world. These religions, as well as, some of their practices have penetrated many aspects of modern life everywhere. People who use the religious lingo or take part in the spiritual practices might not claim to be a member of an Eastern religion, but it just goes to show how religious concepts can seep into and influence our lives.

In this chapter, we will research the beliefs and practices of Hinduism, Buddhism and Confucianism. The largest population demographics of the world are found in the East. China is the most populated country in the world and India is in a very tight second place. The three religions listed above are practiced by large percentages of the people living in the East. For example, in 2017, 79% of a population of 1.3 billion people in India practice Hinduism. That is roughly 1 billion practicing Hindus.[91] Buddhism began in India, but they only comprise about 1% of Buddhists. On the other hand, 80% of the Chinese population, or over 1 billion people, claim to be Buddhists.[92]

---

[91] http://www.indiaonlinepages.com/population/hindu-population-in-india.html
[92] https://buddhaweekly.com/buddhism-now-2nd-largest-spiritual-path-1-6-billion-22-worlds-population-according-recent-studies/

HINDUISM

Let's start with the religion of Hinduism because, after Christianity and Islam, it is the third largest religion in the world. Hinduism has no true founder or definitive historical beginnings, but it is thought to have begun around 1500 B.C. This was the time in history when the Aryans invaded the Indus River Valley and mixed their culture and beliefs with the Dravidians.[93] Three fundamental principles came as a result: the belief in reincarnation, the worship of diverse gods and the belief in the spiritual unity of mankind. Pantheism became the norm, meaning the belief that god is the world and the world is god. This culminates into everything being divine. There is a phrase in Hinduism which states, *"All is one, all is god."*

Hinduism is different from all of the other religions we have covered so far, in that it is a collection of beliefs that derived from Indian culture and allows the adherents to choose whether they want to worship one god, multiple gods or even no god at all. The ultimate goal of Hinduism is to achieve liberation from the bondage of the birth-death cycle and become one with the Universal Soul or Brahman. Brahma is the creator god and the number one god in Hinduism. If one is released from bondage, it is known as achieving *moksha*, salvation or enlightenment.

But there are other methods in the Hindu religion which help one to achieve moksha. One is *dharma*, meaning "law," "teaching" and "religion" in the Sanskrit language. Dharma essentially means fulfilling one's destiny or purpose. *Artha* is

---

[93] *World Religions and Cults 101,* Bruce Bickel and Stan Jantz, Harvest House Publishers, 2002, pages 150-151

another goal of Hinduism, which is the pursuit of wealth and prosperity. And the goal of *kama* is pleasure and enjoyment sexually, as well as, in other life pursuits.

The Vedas is the original holy book of Hinduism. It is believed by Hindus to be supernaturally inspired. There are three popular gods in Hinduism: Brahma, Vishnu, who is incarnated as Krishna, and Shiva. The major majority of Hindus worship one or more of these gods.

The worship of Brahma created an entire caste system in India. The Brahmin priests, who took care of the temple and rituals, became very powerful by creating a complicated system of social classes, as well as, rules of the caste system, known as *Varna*. Of course, the priests secured the highest positions as *Brahmins*. They were followed by *Kshatriyas*, or warriors and rulers. Next were the *Vaisyas*, or merchants and artists. Below the Vaisyas were *Shudras*, or slaves. Within each of these four castes were hundreds of subcategories. Only the top three castes were allowed to practice Hinduism.[94]

By 500 B.C., the oppression created by the caste system caused some to break away from Hinduism. Buddhism was created out of this reform movement. Also, another set of Hindu scriptures, called the *Upanishad*, gained popularity among the followers of Brahma. The Vedas writings focused on inner meditation rather than outward performance, but the Upanishad introduced spiritual instructors, or *gurus*, into Hinduism. "Guru" means "to sit near to." The school of thought that formed out of the Upanishad was known as *Vedanta* and encouraged unity in diversity.

---

[94] *World Religions and Cults 101*, Bruce Bickel and Stan Jantz, Harvest House Publishers, 2002, page 153

Vedanta influenced beliefs in reincarnation, or *samsara*. Hindus believe that there is an individual soul, called *atman*, and then there is a Universal Soul, or *Brahman*. As already stated, Brahman is the goal of Hinduism, when the individual soul unites with the Universal Soul. In order for this to occur, the atman must die and be reincarnated many times into different bodies. Some even believe that a person can be reincarnated as an animal or plant. Moksha (salvation) will finally take place when the samsara (reincarnation) cycle ends and the atman (individual soul) is united with the Brahman (Universal Soul).

In order to be reincarnated into a better caste system, Hindus must consider their *karma*. The law of karma weighs good karma against bad karma. Once the individual soul has produced enough good karma, they believe that the reincarnation cycle ceases as the individual soul is united with the Universal Soul. Someone who dies with too much bad karma may be reincarnated as something undesirable. They believe that both good and bad karma can carry over from the previous life.

How can a Hindu attain good karma and eventually moksha? There are three ways or *margas*: the way of activity, the way of knowledge and the way of devotion. *The way of activity* is accomplished by waking up the statue of their god each day, talking to it, bathing it and offering flowers, food and incense.

The way of knowledge is the least popular because it is the most difficult to complete. It involves different stages beginning with the student stage, where the Veda scriptures are studied. Stage two is the householder stage with the act of marriage and raising a family. The third stage is the forest dweller stage where the Hindu gives up property and family to leave home for the forest. He finds a guru and devotes himself to meditation. The last stage is the ascetic stage where the Hindu has learned as much as he can from the guru and is now ready to practice yoga.

On a quick side note, yoga has become all the craze nowadays and it is not confined to India. The purpose of yoga is to release the *kundalini* or *serpent power*. For a Hindu, it helps him approach a mystical union with the Universal Soul.

Here is the significance of "kundalini" in the words of a renowned Hindu Yogi:

- Kundalini (Divine Serpent Power) is a super power of our life. Over here lies focused all energies of the body and mind.
- Great Yogis, Rishis, Munis had discovered it. They all proclaimed that Kundalini is the supreme energy.
- It is the final step that helps us unite with God. Divine Serpent Power is the super power of our life.
- When it is activated, man attains divine knowledge. He can thus become a great poet, artist or scientist.
- Divine Serpent Power is the Mother of material and spiritual philosophy.[95]

Most non-Hindus believe that they are simply doing stretching and relaxation exercises, but it is best to steer clear of any kind of exercise which aims to uncoil the *"divine serpent power"* and claims to be the avenue where one will unite with God. Not only is it unbiblical, but it is extremely dangerous.

The final method to achieve good karma is *the way of devotion*. Hindus can choose from any of the multiple millions of gods available to devote their worship. The most common choice is Vishnu, the god of incarnations. Krishna, the more well-known Hindu god, is considered to be the incarnation of Vishnu. They believe that devotion to Krishna offers relief from the samsara

---

[95] http://www.shriramsharma.com/

cycle through Krishna's love and grace. The way of devotion is the most popular among Hindus in achieving good karma and moving toward moksha.

It is easy to see that Hinduism is nothing like true Christianity as revealed in the Bible. But it has made an impact, not just in India, but all over the world. How many people today practice yoga? How many people meditate on a regular basis? How often does a non-Hindu use the word "mantra?" How many times have you heard someone say, *"karma,"* when you experience a misfortune after committing a not-so-kind act? It just goes to show us how far reaching the Hindu religious culture has permeated everyday life.

BUDDHISM

The religion of Buddhism has a wide appeal because it encourages the awareness of an individual to reach a higher level of enlightenment. The stage of enlightenment is accomplished through morality, meditation and wisdom, with the ultimate goal being a state of *"nirvana."* Earlier we mentioned that the religion of Buddhism came out of Hinduism and that is because the caste system of Hinduism caused a discontented prince to create his own path to enlightenment.

Buddhism was created by Prince Siddhartha Gautama in the 6th century B.C. Siddhartha was not allowed outside of the palace gates because before his birth, a prediction was made to his parents that he would either be a great political leader or, if he witnessed great suffering, he would become a great religious leader. His father was hoping that the pendulum would swing in the political direction, so he kept Siddhartha from leaving the privileged palace gates.

Siddhartha went on to marry and have children, but his curiosity got the best of him and he desired to see the outside world. What he saw on his first short trip caused him to think about old age, sickness, death and the meaning of life. This experience caused Siddhartha to shave his head, leave his family and go into the forest where he met two holy men who taught him meditation. In Buddhism, this episode is known as "The Great Renunciation."

Siddhartha fasted and meditated until he claimed to have an "awakening." During the night, as he meditated under a Bodhi tree, Siddhartha was said to have had an internal battle with Mara, the personification of change, death and evil. By the time morning came, Siddhartha had defeated Mara and awoke with great clarity and an understanding of life. His conclusion was that the superior spiritual path should be a middle ground between unreasonable excess and unnecessary deprivation.

As Siddhartha shared his revelation, he became known as "Buddha," or "the Enlightened One." Buddha died at the age of eighty and it is believed that he had achieved the state of nirvana. Nirvana is when the reincarnation cycle stops, the soul is liberated and suffering finally ends. Since Siddhartha Gautama, the original Buddha, there have been many others who are believed to have reached nirvana and therefore, also became "Buddha."

Buddha was never seen as a god, but as a great teacher and one who taught people how to exit a life of continual suffering. Statues of Buddha are to remind people of the opportunity for enlightenment and are not intended to be used to worship him.

Let us look at some of Buddha's basic precepts and teachings. Buddha encouraged people to live in "the way of the middle," through Four Noble Truths. The first truth is *dukkha*, meaning that life is all about suffering and, unfortunately, it does not end because of the reincarnation cycle. The second truth is *samudaya*, which means that the reason for suffering is because of our own selfish desires and greed. The "three root evils" of greed, hatred and ignorance are considered the root of all sufferings. The third truth is *nirodha*, meaning that there is a way to extinguish the fires of greed, hatred and ignorance and that is by entering the state of nirvana, where the suffering ends. And the fourth and final truth is *marga*, meaning that the path to happiness and relief from suffering is found in the Noble Eightfold Path.

The steps of the Noble Eightfold Path include three qualities. The first is the *Quality of Wisdom*, which is a right understanding of the suffering world and also, right thoughts, which come about through purifying the heart through thoughts of unselfishness and compassion. The second is *Quality of Mental Discipline*, which includes right efforts to prevent evil in the mind; right mindfulness, which is total awareness of the body, mind and speech; and right concentration, which comes about by training the mind through meditation. The third and last quality is *Quality of Ethical Conduct,* which involves right speech or refraining from lying or gossiping; right action, which means to refrain from killing, taking what is not yours, avoiding inappropriate sexual conduct, improper speech and intoxicants; and right livelihood, which means earning a living in a way that does not bring harm to others.[96]

There are not many doctrines or rules in Buddhism, but there are three fundamental principles known as *tiratna*, or the Three Jewels. The first jewel is *Buddha* because he discovered the path of enlightenment and taught it to others. The second jewel is

---

[96] *World Religions and Cults 101,* Bruce Bickel and Stan Jantz, Harvest House Publishers, 2002, page 176

dharma, which is the teaching of the true ways of life. And the third jewel is *sanga*, which is the community of monks, nuns and laymen who practice and promote dharma.

There are two main sects of Buddhism and they both accept each other's paths to enlightenment. The first is Buddhist of Tibet, known as *Mahayana*. These dwell in the regions of Tibet and northern Asia, which includes China and Japan. They espouse diverse methods to nirvana and recognize the critical role of the *bodhisattva*, which is a person who is destined to reach nirvana.

A bodhisattva is a person who has delayed reaching nirvana intentionally, so that he can teach others the pathway of understanding. They follow a path based on six perfections and promise to be perfectly generous, virtuous, patient, energetic, meditative and wise. The most famous bodhisattva is the Dalai Lama, who the Tibetan Buddhist believe to be the reincarnated Avalokiteshvara.

Tibetan Buddhist use a *mantra* to achieve the meditative state. A mantra can be a single sound or a repetitive phrase that empties the mind and brings on a trance-like state needed for meditation.

The second sect of Buddhism is Buddhist of Southeast Asia, called *Theravada*, meaning "Doctrine of the Elders." Theravada are seen as more of the conservative branch of Buddhism and are found concentrated in Southeast Asia and Sri Lanka. There is an interdependent relationship between Theravada monks and the laymen. The monks are supported by the community with offerings of food and clothing, while they teach and train the laymen. It is very unlikely that a laymen will reach nirvana, so the goal is to be reincarnated into a monk or nun in the next life.

Theravada monks live according to Ten Precepts, which means that they refrain from: harming any living thing; taking what is not given; inappropriate sexual relations; wrong speech;

intoxicating drugs or drink; eating after the midday meal; dancing, music, singing and unseemly shows; garlands, perfumes and personal adornments; using comfortable chairs or beds; or accepting gold or silver.

Meditation is central to Buddhism because this practice is considered to be the path to understanding the truth about the nature of reality. Meditation is the means for obtaining dharma, the understanding of life. Through meditation, the Buddhist seeks to awaken a source of spiritual power from within.

Like Hinduism, Buddhism also teaches that karma plays a role in the reincarnation process. The difference is that in Hinduism, the good karma is achieved through works and in Buddhism, the good karma is achieved by an inward journey of renunciation of the world as we know it and shifting their morals to a place where they make the world a better place. It is a total self-dependence on their own individual morality.

There is no god in Buddhism, no higher power, and no holy book, just an individual's own struggle to attain nirvana through the reincarnation cycle and end the suffering of the present life. Needless to say, Buddhism is reliance of self to attain their version of Heaven, which is nirvana. However, nirvana is not a promise of an eternal life in a glorious place, but has been best described as the flame of a candle being extinguished forever.

CONFUCIANISM

The last religion we will probe in this chapter is Confucianism, which originated in the 6th century B.C. by K'ung Fu Tzu, or "Confucius" in the English language. He was born in the midst of the great dynasties of the Shantung Province of China in an upper class family and was considered to be a rebel of his time.

During this time, the desire for wisdom was being replaced with the desire for great wealth. This era was famous for its lack of civility and loose morals, which Confucius rejected and instead blazed a path of morality, integrity and decency.

He believed that *"resistance to change was futile,"* and felt that if society was not kept in check, that it would eventually deteriorate to a state of barbarism. His personal mission was to change society through better moral conduct before it was too late. Confucius believed that the character of the ruler could influence the nature of his citizens. He spent much of his life traveling and advising rulers on ethical standards of government which changed the entire course of Chinese society.

The religion of Confucianism emphasizes the question of the ultimate meaning of life. There is no god and not many doctrines of faith, but it based on a belief system of ethical behavior in dealing with different relationships that a person will encounter in a lifetime. It runs the gamut from how governments should treat citizens to one-on-one personal relationships. The five ethical relationships to consider are: the parent-child relationship; the relationship between rulers and their subjects; the husband-wife relationship; the relationship between siblings; and the relationship between friends.

Confucius emphasized certain ethical values which should be applied in the most important relationships of life: *Li*, proper conduct and etiquette; *Hsiao*, love between family members; *Yi*, righteousness, decency and virtue; *Xin*, honesty and trustworthiness; *Jen*, kindness toward others; and *Chung*, loyalty and faithfulness.

The teachings of Confucius were compiled into nine books and after his death and his verbal wisdoms rapidly spread. Unfortunately, Confucius was in the middle of writing several books when he died, causing some questions left unanswered. This sparked two schools of thought: The Mencius (371-289 B.C.) and the Xunzi (300-230 B.C.).

Mencius believed that people were inherently good and their own intuition should be a guide to morally upright behavior. He believed that government should be structured to allow the "good" majority prevail, which would produce a benevolent government. On the other hand, Xunzi taught that humans were born with an evil nature and because of this fact, a strict code of conduct and ethics must be applied to help them become righteous. He concentrated on preventing the negative behaviors and using them as a way to turn people from evil to good.

Although there was not a contest between these two teachings, Mencius' teachings prevailed over that of Xunzi. Traditional Confucianism adopted Mencius' pattern that each individual has the potential to achieve the four virtues: humanity, righteousness, propriety and wisdom. This statement summarizes these virtues:

> All things are within me, and on self-examination, I find no greater joy than to be true to myself. We should do our best to treat others as we wish to be treated. Nothing is more appropriate than to seek after goodness.[97]

Confucianism has changed over the long centuries since its inception. There are different forms of Confucianism today, such as neo-Confucianism, contemporary neo-Confucianism and also territorial Confucianism, such as Japanese, Korean, and

---

[97] *World Religions and Cults 101,* Bruce Bickel and Stan Jantz, Harvest House Publishers, 2002, page 195

Singaporean. But, despite the different alterations, Confucianism remains to be a system of thought by which civilized behavior is stressed for the benefit of the significant relationships one will encounter over a lifetime. Again, there is no god, certainly no Jesus Christ and there is really no redemption plan or afterlife at all. People that practice Confucianism are placing the focus on themselves to achieve everything that the religion expects of them, with no promise of an eternal future in Heaven, only a good life in the present.

Chapter Thirteen

THE NOT SO "NEW" AGE
& HER COLLEAGUES

The New Age began at the turn of the 20th century, but since the dawn of the new millennium, it has truly exploded. We see New Age practices in all aspects of society today, including business, healthcare, science, politics, entertainment and even sports. Why? Because within the New Age, there is a focus on healthy living, respect for the planet, inner peace and harmony in the world. New Age supporters emphasize self-actualization, spiritual awareness, enlightenment and global spiritual unity, as well as, global political unity.

It was Alice Bailey who popularized the term "New Age" in the early 1900's and the new age that she referred to was the "Age of Aquarius." She believed that this began shortly after the turn of the 20th century and claimed that the Age of Aquarius was when human beings would recognize *the god within themselves.*"[98]

Within the New Age, there is no creed, no particular founder, no central church headquarters or a formal structure of any kind. It is a hybrid mixture of many belief systems including Hinduism, Buddhism, Taoism, Gnosticism, Native Americanism

---

[98] http://www.lighthousetrailsresearch.com/alicebailey.htm

and Occultism with a strong emphasis on Spiritism. Here is a list of characteristics of New Age beliefs:[99]

- *Syncretism:* The combination of many different systems of religious and philosophical beliefs and practices.
- *Monism:* The belief that we are all one in unity.
- *Pantheism:* The belief that God is in everything, making everything divine.
- *Divinity of man:* The belief that humans have the potential to become gods themselves because they are a part of God.
- *Enlightenment:* Personal transformation, which comes about as man recognizes the god within himself and becomes one with the Universe. The final stage of this transformation is referred to as "enlightenment" or "self-actualization."
- *Worship of Mother Earth:* New agers worship creation instead of the Creator. Monism and pantheism create the idea that because everything is divine, it should be all be worshipped.
- *New World Order:* This concept is that the New Age can usher in a New World Order, where there will be peace in a unified global society with a one world government. The Bible speaks of this same concept, except it describes this New World Order as the kingdom of the Antichrist (Revelation 13: 7).

The chapter title of "the not so 'New' Age" was chosen because the roots of the New Age Movement extend way back to the Garden of Eden. How? Well, Lucifer is esteemed and worshiped by Luciferians and New Agers because they believe that he was responsible for the "spiritual liberation of mankind." They

---

[99] *World Religions and Cults 101,* Bruce Bickel and Stan Jantz, Harvest House Publishers, 2002, pages 219-220

teach that God was holding mankind in spiritual bondage, until Lucifer intervened in the Garden of Eden and released Adam and Eve from God's oppressive stronghold. Helena Petrovna Blavatsky, founder of the Theosophical Society and an inspiration to the New Age religion, wrote in her book, *The Secret Doctrine*:

> In this case it is but natural...to view Satan, the Serpent of Genesis as the real creator and benefactor, the Father of Spiritual Mankind... Stand in awe of him, and sin not, speak his name with trembling... It is Satan who is the god of our planet and the only god...[100]

Where did Helena Blavatsky receive her ideas which ultimately became very influential in the New Age Movement? She was born in 1831 of German nobility into the von Hahn family. Blavatsky moved often in her youth, but mainly lived in Russia, where she immersed herself at a young age into occult writings. She openly confided to a friend about:

> ...her future participation in the work which some day would serve to liberate the human mind.[101]

> This work is not mine, *but he who sends me* (My italics).[102]

Blavatsky became an American citizen and founded the Theosophical Society in New York City in 1875. The objectives

---

[100] *The Secret Doctrine,* Helena Petrovna Blavatsky, Volume II, page 235
[101] http://en.wikipedia.org/wiki/Helena_Blavatsky
[102] http://en.wikipedia.org/wiki/Helena_Blavatsky

of the Theosophical Society were threefold:

- The first was to 'form a nucleus of the Universal Brotherhood of Humanity, without distinction of race, creed, sex, caste, or color.'
- The second goal was 'to encourage the study of comparative religion, philosophy, and science.'
- And last was 'to investigate the unexplained laws of nature and the powers latent in man.'[103]

Madame Blavatsky, as she was known, explained that "theosophy" was defined as *the divine knowledge and wisdom of the gods.*" She received her teachings and ideas from her contact with a spirit guide, whom she referred to as "her Teacher."

Blavatsky was also influential in modern Buddhism, as well as, Hindu reform movements. Although she died in 1891, Blavatsky had a very strong impact in what would become the New Age Movement. Her writings: *The Secret Doctrine, Isis Unveiled, The Key to Theosophy* and *The Voice of Silence* are still revered by New Agers today.

Blavatsky's teachings influenced Alice Bailey, who was mentioned earlier for coining the phrase, "New Age." Bailey greatly impacted the New Age Movement with her many writings. She was born Alice LaTrobe Bateman in 1880 and grew up in the Anglican Church of England, but eventually became active in the Theosophical Society after having been introduced to Blavatsky's writings.[104] As a member of the Theosophical Society, Bailey learned to participate in Eastern meditation, as well as, to channel

---

[103] http://en.wikipedia.org/wiki/Helena_Blavatsky
[104] http://en.wikipedia.org/wiki/Alice_Bailey

spirit guides.

In 1919, Alice Bailey was asked by a "voice" to write a series of books and she finally agreed after hearing from her master spirit guide that it would be a *really valuable piece of work.*[105] She described the majority of her work as having been telepathically dictated to her by a Master of Wisdom, referred to as "the Tibetan," "D.K.," or "Djwal Khul."

Between 1919 and 1949, Alice Bailey wrote nineteen books by means of her telepathic communication with D.K. and then another seven books on her own.[106] She and her second husband, Foster Bailey, created a publishing company, which they named "Lucifer Trust." This publishing company still exists today as "Lucis Trust."[107]

Lucifer Trust published all of Alice Bailey's writings. Her books focused on the anticipation of a world healer and savior who would unite all of mankind under his guidance, as well as, unite the religions of the East and the West. She called him the "coming one." This was not to be Jesus Christ, but an entirely different person who would supposedly be the "perfection of man." Bailey writes:

> The coming one will not be Christian, a Hindu, a Buddhist, not an American, Jew, Italian or Russian. His title is not important; he is for all humanity, to unite all religions, philosophies and nations.[108]

---

[105] http://www.share-berlin.info/bailey.htm
[106] *A Time of Departing*, Ray Yungen, Lighthouse Trails Publishing Co., Oregon, 2006, pg. 112
[107] http://www.lucistrust.org/
[108] *A Time of Departing*, Ray Yungen, Lighthouse Trails Publishing Co., Oregon, 2006, page 114

Any person who studies eschatology will shudder at this statement, because it describes the **"man of perdition,"** or the Antichrist of the Bible, very well. The following quotation outlines the profound impression Alice Bailey has made on today's New Age spirituality:

> Her vision of a unified society includes a global 'spirit of religion' different from traditional religious forms and including the concept of the Age of Aquarius. Bailey taught a form of universal spirituality that transcended denominational identification, believing that: 'Every class of human beings is a group of brothers. Catholics, Jews, Gentiles, Occidentals and Orientals are all the sons of God.' She stated that all religions originate from the same spiritual source, and that humanity will eventually come to realize this, and as they do so, the result will be the emergence of a universal world religion and a 'new world order.'[109]

Both Helena Blavatsky and Alice Bailey relied heavily on spirit guides for direction and inspiration in their writings. What are "spirit guides?" They are Lucifer's fallen angels, who sided with his rebellion and were cast out of Heaven sometime in eternity past. These spirit guides work continually through men and woman to fulfill Lucifer's desires to be the god of this world. Those who do not read the Word of God can easily be misled by these tactics.

---

[109] http://en.wikipedia.org/wiki/Alice_Bailey

Based on historical facts, the New Age is an offshoot of Luciferian worship. I make this statement because the inspiration and founders of the New Age, Blavatsky and Bailey, both openly gave obeisance to Lucifer. They both considered him to be the *"Father of Spiritual Mankind,"* and Alice Bailey went as far as to name her publishing company "Lucifer Trust."

This quote by David Spangler, a New Age activist and Director of Planetary Initiative United Nations, makes the New Age mission crystal clear. He said:

> No one will enter the New World Order... unless he or she will make a pledge to worship Lucifer. No one will enter the New Age unless he will take a Luciferian Initiation.[110]

LUCIFERIANSIM & SATANISM

Is Luciferianism a religion? Yes, because it meets the benchmarks for such a label. Luciferians, as stated previously, believe that Lucifer was the benevolent protagonist who saved mankind from God's stronghold in the Garden of Eden. Here is an explanation of this religion from a Luciferian approved website:

Luciferianism is the ideological, philosophical and Magickial attainment of knowledge and inner power via the left hand path. The type of knowledge sought is firstly that of the self: strengths, weaknesses and all that which makes us truly 'individual'. Initiation or the

---

[110] http://quotes.liberty-tree.ca/quote_blog/David.Spangler.Quote.ACEF

revealing of knowledge is through study, practicing Adversarial Magick/Sorcery and the continual struggle for self-improvement through spiritual rebellion.

The left hand path for Luciferians *is not a specific doctrine* yet clearly an aspect of who we are. Luciferians are against the social concept of 'God' and 'Religion' as both is collective, sheep-herding doctrines which suppress knowledge, reward weakness and apathy and place unrealistic expectations on the individual for a 'future' reward which <u>does not exist</u>. Luciferians do not accept the dualistic concept of 'good' and 'evil'; we hold the opinion that like in nature, darkness empowers light and light establishes growth and renewal.

Luciferians do not believe in an 'afterlife' in the way which Judeo-Christians do. This does not insinuate that Luciferians don't believe in the possibility or existence of an afterlife, there is just no need to believe in the Judeo-Christian absolutes such as a blissful paradise or some horrid place of punishment where terrible demons continually torture those who do not recognize the executed criminal-turned savior (Jesus) and his perceived 'father (God)'. In short, you will be hard pressed to find a Luciferian who believes in the 'devil' and in 'hell' (My notes in parentheses).[111]

Are Luciferianism and Satanism the same? While the Bible conveys that Lucifer and Satan are one in the same, Luciferians and Satanists do not see him as the same entity. Satan

---

[111] https://www.luciferianapotheca.com/pages/luciferianism-an-introduction

is seen as the symbol of carnality, materiality and rebellion, while Lucifer is seen as a spiritual and enlightened being.[112]

While Luciferianism and Satanism are both highly individualized religions with no single set of doctrines or rules, they both reject dogmatic religions and see humans as gods having dominion over the planet. Both incorporate magic into their rituals as a means to achieve knowledge, power and godhood.

In Satanism, Satan is seen as a symbol of personal freedom and individuality, and can help one become a god. From the Church of Satan's website:

> Our members champion personal development and rejection of herd conformity, and thus each Satanist finds his own unique path to self-deification.[113]

Satanism requires horrendous acts of violence against young boys and girls. Malachi Martin explains why Satanic Ritual Abuse (SRA) is so common, in *The Keys of This Blood*:

> The cultic acts of Satanic pedophilia are considered by professionals to be the culmination (or the highest phase) of the Fallen Archangel's (Lucifer's) rites.[114]

---

[112] https://www.thoughtco.com/how-luciferians-differ-from-satanists-95678
[113] https://www.churchofsatan.com/history.php
[114] *The Keys of This Blood*, Malachi Martin, page 278

HUMANISTIC PSYCHOLOGY

Around the same time the New Age religion was heating up for massive impact, another movement was brewing. While it is not an official religion, it has certainly become a religion of its own to some. I am speaking of Humanistic Psychology, which has been an antidote to many who are troubled in life. In order to understand Humanistic Psychology, it is best to look at its origins.

The "father of psychotherapy," Sigmund Freud, died about twenty years into the New Age Movement. Freud made great strides in the analysis of the mind and of the unconscious psyche. He was a very disturbed individual in many areas of his life. He freely admitted to having sexual desires for his own birth mother and to having numerous psychosomatic disorders in which he suffered with during his lifetime.[115] His own drug of choice for his manic depression was cocaine, which he often recommended to his own patients.[116] Freud was Jewish by birth, but he professed to be an atheist.[117] He had no use for God because his beliefs were that man could fix his own problems through psychotherapy.

Another "father of the science of the mind" was Carl Jung, the founder of Analytical Psychology. He was described as *"a solitary and introverted child who was convinced that he had two separate personalities."* Jung was forcibly separated from his own mother at an early age because she was *"an eccentric and depressed woman"* who spent much of her time in her own separate bedroom, *"enthralled by the spirits"* that she said *"visited her in the*

---

night."[118] Jung also had many spirit guides, one of which called himself, "Philemon."[119] He was heavily influenced by his travels to India where he:

> ...became fascinated and deeply involved with Eastern philosophies and religions, helping him come up with key concepts of his ideology, including integrating spirituality into everyday life and the appreciation of the unconscious.[120]

Here we have two of the key forces in the development of Humanistic Psychology; one a professed Atheist and the other deeply involved with Eastern religious practices and channeled spirit guides. When researching Satanism, books by Carl Jung and Sigmund Freud were recommended non-fiction reading for the Church of Satan. Anton LaVey, the founder of the Church of Satan, openly endorsed both men's writings.[121]

All of this information should be taken into consideration in understanding that *psychology is not of God.* The truth is that psychology is "man fixing man," and it will never be able to completely cure man of his problems because it takes God out of the picture. Most importantly, Humanistic Psychology teaches that there is no soul or spirit and that the human body is biological matter that will die and eventually nothing will remain.

---

[118] http://www.answers.com/topic/carl-jung
[119] http://www.philipcoppens.com/jung.html
[120] http://en.wikipedia.org/wiki/Carl_Jung
[121] https://www.churchofsatan.com/sources-book-list.php

AGNOSTICISM & ATHEISM

The last "religions" we will deal with in this chapter are Agnosticism and Atheism. While these factions may not consider themselves to be religions per se, this book will classify them as such because Atheists and Agnostics are cohesive groups of people who ban together in their particular belief systems. Also, both are well formed groups of individuals which are growing in number every day.

First, let us study the Agnostic view of God. Theism is the belief in the existence of one or more divine beings, but Agnosticism claims that there is not enough evidence to support the existence of God. An Agnostic uses the intellectual position of not taking a stand one way or the other on the existence or non-existence of God. They fall somewhere in between Theistic and Atheistic beliefs. The term "Agnostic" was coined in 1869 during debates over Western biblical beliefs and the scientific evolutionary theories of Charles Darwin.[122]

On the other hand, Atheism denies the existence of any supernatural beings or any meaning to the Universe. They take the stand that "God" is a fictitious concept and was created in the mind of man. There are two divisions within Atheism: A weak-position Atheist or negative Atheism and a strong-position Atheist or positive Atheism.

The weak-position Atheist believes that there is no God, but they also agree that while God may exist, they personally have not yet been convinced of this fact. In this mindset, others are free

---

[122] *World Religions and Cults 101,* Bruce Bickel and Stan Jantz, Harvest House Publishers, 2002, pages 234-235

to believe what they want about God. But, in strong-position Atheism, it has been concluded, without a shadow of a doubt, that God does not exist. They adamantly refuse to be convinced otherwise and will not debate over the existence of a God who they believe does not exist in the first place.

Because Atheist do not believe in the existence of God, they believe that mankind was not created, but came about randomly as a part of the evolutionary process of nature. Man uses his intelligence to stay on the tip top of the food chain. And, because there is no God, then sin does not exist either. An Atheist recognizes that some things are bad, but does not attach any eternal consequences to these actions.

Atheism teaches that there is no afterlife or salvation available to humans after death. They believe that man lives and then once he dies, the life is over with no soul or spirit to live on eternally. There are no absolute standards of right or wrong in Atheism, so morally, an Atheist can do whatever he wants to do, short of what society considers illegal. They believe that the Bible is a book of fables, and that if Jesus ever did actually exist, He certainly was not God.

There were many belief systems covered in this chapter, with the main focus being the New Age religion. All of these have one major ideology in common: God is either disregarded, or completely denied. But the interesting thing is that when God is taken out of the picture, something must fill the void. In the case of all of these religions, that void is "self." The focus of "self" became the Achilles heel of Adam and Eve in the Garden of Eden and, unfortunately, many people have followed suit. Remember, though, this notion of self-actualization came directly from the Serpent of Genesis!

Chapter Fourteen

DOCTRINES, TRADITIONS & COMMANDMENTS OF MEN

Jesus cautions us in Mark 7: 7, 8, 13, when He says, **"Howbeit in vain do they worship Me, teaching doctrines and commandments of men. For laying aside the commandments of God, you hold the tradition of men... Making the Word of God of none effect by your traditions."** Making something **"of none effect"** means to make it obsolete. Jesus is saying here that the doctrines, traditions and commandments of men completely contradict the Word of God.

Likely, we've all heard the phrase, *"If you don't stand for something, you will fall for anything."* Well, how do we know what to "stand for," so that we won't "fall for anything?" Everyone, everywhere is searching for truth. The problem is that unless we have a baseline for truth, we will likely believe what we have been taught to believe or we will conjure up our own idea of truth, derived from feelings and life experiences.

I have already stated that I was baptized into the Roman Catholic Church at ten days old, attended Roman Catholic school for thirteen years and taught in a Roman Catholic School for ten years. I took my "truth" from what I grew up hearing and learning. As a Roman Catholic, we were required to either attend Roman Catholic school or attend a weekly Catechism class at the local church. In religion classes, the focus was learning about the beliefs of Roman Catholicism. It was not about the Bible, or what the

Bible teaches. In my thirty-two years as a Roman Catholic, I don't remember *ever* even opening a Bible.

My beliefs came from the doctrines, traditions and commandments of men. Because this is the religion that I was raised in, I believed that it was superior to others and that it was correct. Most people will say the same of whatever belief system they grew up in, unless the Holy Spirit shows them otherwise. I thank God that He showed me the path to truth and then backed it up with His written Word, the Bible.

There comes a time in each of our lives when we have to search for ourselves to find truth. At some point in our lives, God will deal with each and every one of us concerning truth and the salvation of our eternal souls. We must be sensitive to the Holy Spirit, because He is one who draws us to the truth of salvation and points us to Jesus Christ. Unfortunately, not everyone will heed the call of the Holy Spirit, but those who do will be eternally grateful.

What about the expression: *"follow your heart."* While that sounds fulfilling, Jeremiah said, **"the heart is deceitful above all things, and desperately wicked, who can know it (Jeremiah 17: 9)?"** Remember, because of Adam's fall, we were born with the inherent sin nature, so listening to our own corrupted hearts might not be the best advice. So, what is a person to do? Where can we find real solid truth?

Jesus gave us a hint when He said, **"I am the way, the truth and the life, no man comes unto the Father, but by Me (John 14: 6)."** Jesus also said, **"To this end was I born, and for this cause came I into the world, that I should bear witness unto the truth. Every one that is of the truth hears my voice."**

We have already stated that Jesus is the Word of God because He fulfilled the Old Covenant by keeping the Mosaic Law perfectly (John 1: 1, 14, 29). *The Jehovah of the Old Covenant is the Jesus of the New Covenant.* The ultimate "truth" portrayed in the

Bible is that Jesus came for the expressed purpose of going to the Cross to save mankind from the effects of the Fall of Man. We can only find this truth in the Holy Scriptures.

Isaiah 28: 10 says, **"For precept must be upon precept... line upon line; here a little, and there a little..."** This means that *everything must be measured by the Word of God.* Paul stressed the importance of the Scriptures in 2 Timothy 3: 15-16 when he said, **"And that from a child you have known the Holy Scriptures, which are able to make you wise unto salvation through faith which is in Christ Jesus. All Scripture *is* given by inspiration of God, and is profitable for doctrine, for reproof, for correction, for instruction in righteousness..."** How can Paul claim that **"All Scripture is given by inspiration of God..."**?

Paul writes this because the Bible was written by people chosen by God and under the inspiration of the Holy Spirit. It provides proof that Jesus was born, was crucified on the Cross and was resurrected from the dead three days later. Jerusalem, today, still contains this historical evidence and people travel from all over the world to visit. The cities, mountains and rivers mentioned in the Bible still exist today, although some of the names have been changed over time. Some will attempt to claim that the Bible is only a book of allegorical stories, but it is the only Book of its kind that contains historical evidence for real events in real places with real people who actually existed. No other "sacred" writings can boast this claim.

It is true that the Bible has been translated many different times over the centuries in order to obtain new copyrights and also, by some, to remove important verses which would cause people to question their religion's belief system.[123] But, God promised that His Word would be preserved for all generations in Psalms 12: 6-7 where it says, **"The words of the LORD are pure words: as silver tried in a furnace of Earth, purified seven times. You shall keep them, O LORD, You shall preserve them from this generation forever."**

There has only been one translation today which has stood up to God's standards and that is the King James Version Bible. It is a *word for word* translation from the original Hebrew and Greek Received Text. This translating process began in 1611 by approximately fifty Hebrew and Greek scholars at the insistence of King James.[124] It took them seven long years to complete the project because the exchange of languages was taken very seriously. Because the Greek and Hebrew languages have fewer words than the English language, the translators italicized any added words to show that they were not in the original text.

The Dead Sea Scrolls, which were discovered in a cave near Jericho in 1947, provided proof that the King James Version Bible was an accurate translation.[125] Some other versions and translations of the Bible have been paraphrased or have even had Scriptures added or taken out. The Word of God addresses this in Revelation 22: 18-19, where it warns, **"For I testify unto every man who hears the words of the Prophecy of this Book, If any man shall add unto these things, God shall add unto him the plagues that are written in this Book: And if any man shall take away from the words of the Book of this Prophecy, God**

---

[123] For more information, please see my book, *Taking the Bait*, 2017, chapter 11- A One World Bible
[124] http://www.av1611.org/kjv/kjvhist.html
[125] http://www.chick.com/reading/books/158/158_36.asp

shall take away his part out of the Book of Life, and out of the Holy City, and from the things which are written in this Book." The repercussions for changing God's Word are clearly given in this verse. Woe unto them who do not heed this warning.

The Bible is the Holy Book of true Christianity and is inspired by the Holy Spirit to contain truth for all of humanity. It is the only Book claiming to be written by God Himself. There are sixty-six Books of the Bible that are considered to be the inspired canon of Scripture. The word "canon" comes from the word "reed," which was a measuring instrument used in ancient times. Isn't that interesting considering that we should measure everything by the Word of God?

There are approximately 2,500 prophecies given in the Bible, with 2,000 of them having already been fulfilled and the other 500 to come to pass during the future Great Tribulation and second coming of Jesus Christ. Only the Bible has a 100% accuracy rate thus far, showing that it was indeed inspired by God and written by men under the powerful anointing of the Holy Spirit.

The Bible is readily available today to the majority of the world and has changed more lives than we could ever imagine. What about the other "holy" books used by some of the religions covered in the last few chapters? Where do they come from, who wrote them and do they contain the same truth of the Bible?

Before we answer, we must first deal with the fact that truth is absolutely 100% *objective*. Truth does not depend on man's subjective view of creation, humanity, morals and self-driven ideals. There is a yardstick for measuring truth and that is by the Word of God. All other "holy" books we will cover were written by men and completely contradict the Bible.

So, either the Bible is false, or the other "holy" books are lies. Numbers 23: 19 states, **"God is not a man that He should lie; neither the son of man that He should repent: hath He said, and shall He not do it? Or hath He spoken, and shall He** not make it good?" On the contrary, Jesus said in John 8: 44 concerning Satan that he **"...abode not in the truth, because there is no truth in him. When he speaks a lie, he speaks of his own: for he is a liar, and the father of it."**

JUDAISM

Let us first deal with the Holy Books of Judaism. Because Christianity came out of Judaism, there are many books used by the Jews which are indeed the inspired canon of Scripture. The *Written Torah* refers to the entirety of the Jewish law and teachings. Judaism properly views the thirty-nine Books of the Old Testament, or the *Tanakh*, as inspired Scriptures. However, a religious Jew will not accept the New Testament because, as we have already stated on many occasions, they do not believe that Jesus Christ was the Messiah. Because the New Testament is the story of Jesus' incarnation and death on the Cross, it is of no consequence to the religion of Judaism.

The Books of the Tanakh are not ordered as that of the Old Testament. The first five Books of Moses are "the Law," and the other thirty-four Books are categorized as "the Prophets" and "the Writings."

The *Oral Torah* is believed to be the oral teachings passed down from Moses to God's chosen people and has been compiled into the *Talmud*. The Talmud is composed of the *Mishnah* and the *Gemara*, which were books transcribed in the early centuries. The Talmud covers every aspect of life for the Jew and holds the answers to how to deal with all issues of life.

While many of the Jewish books contain truth, unfortunately many of the Jews of Jesus' day, as well as, scores of Jewish people down through the centuries, have disregarded the thousands of prophecies concerning the Messiah. Because of this, they have brought much sorrow and persecution onto their people. But, Zechariah warned God's chosen people that there will come a time when **"They shall look upon Me whom they have pierced, and they shall mourn for Him, as one mourns for his only son, and shall be in bitterness for Him, as one that is in bitterness for his firstborn** (Zechariah 12: 10)**."** This will be fulfilled at the second coming of Jesus Christ and the Jews will finally take their rightful place in God's Kingdom. This is what God had planned for them with Jesus' first advent, until they rejected the chosen Messiah and called for His crucifixion.

ISLAM

The "holy" books of the religion of Islam are comprised of four sacred writings. The first is the *Torah*, the Books of Moses. The second is the *Zabur*, the Psalms of David. The third is the *Injil*, or the Gospels of Jesus Christ. And the last is their most important book, the *Qur'an*, which is the revelation of Muhammad, recited to his transcribers.

Muslims believe that Allah is the author of the Qur'an and that Muhammad was the channel of these revelations. Because the Qur'an was Allah's final message to his people, it replaces all previous revelations, including the Bible. If there is any conflict among the four sacred writings, then the Qur'an's interpretation always prevails. We see this often from offshoots of Christianity, which will claim that the Bible is outdated and that their "prophet" or founder has a fresh new revelation from God.

Despite the fact that some of the sacred books of Islam are trustworthy, Muslims believe that the Jewish Torah and the Gospels of Jesus Christ were misinterpreted by Jews and

Christians and, therefore, are corrupted. In contrast, the Qur'an is seen as perfectly preserved. Please keep in mind that Muhammad did not actually write the Qur'an. After his death, his followers worked tirelessly to collect all of Muhammad's teachings from all over the Middle East and compile them into one book. Also, there have been new revelations, besides that of Muhammad, which were added after his death.

There are other important Islamic books on written tradition which exist. *Sunnah* are the sayings of Muhammad in displaying his conduct toward his followers. These sayings were put into the *Hadith*. The *Qiyas* is an agreement of the Muslim community on interpretations of the Qur'an and the Hadith. And *Shari'ah* is a code of conduct for Muslims, also known as *Shari'ah Law*. This includes many laws and the consequences for breaking them.

Overall, the Qur'an contradicts the Word of God and uses a warped view of the many biblical figures we read about in the legitimate Bible. Sura 5: 51 of the Quran states, *"Believers, take not Jews and Christians for your friends..."* The Qur'an calls for Islamic world dominance and absolutely no tolerance for "infidels." It is certainly a far cry from the Bible, which teaches us to **"love one another"** as God has loved us (John 15: 12).

One of the most glaring differences to the God of the Bible and the god of Islam is that God has unconditional love for His creation, while Allah is only a god of judgment and displays no love for his people. That contradiction alone should be enough to prove that the "holy" books of Islam are man-made and not Holy Spirit inspired books.

ROMAN CATHOLICISM

When it comes to Roman Catholicism, or "the Mother," as she was described in Chapter 10, let us look directly to the *Catechism of the Catholic Church* to find her final authority: [126]

> It is clear therefore that, in the supremely wise arrangement of God, sacred Tradition, Sacred Scripture, and the Magisterium of the Church are so connected and associated that one of them cannot stand without the others. Working together, each on its own way, under the action of the one Holy Spirit, they all contribute effectively to the salvation of souls.

> Sacred Scripture is the speech of God as it is put down in writing under the breath of the Holy Spirit, And (Holy) Tradition transmits in its entirely the Word of God which has been entrusted to the apostles by Christ our Lord and the Holy Spirit.

> The task of giving an authentic interpretation of the Word of God, whether in its written form or in the form of Tradition, has been entrusted to the living teaching office of the Church (Magisterium) alone. This means that the task of interpretation has been entrusted to the bishops in communion with the successor of Peter, the Bishop of Rome (the pope).

---

[126] *Catechism of the Catholic Church*, 1994, page 29 # 95; page 26 #81; page 27 #85

Of course, when the *Catechism of the Catholic Church* refers to *"the Church"* and the *"Magisterium of the Church,"* it is referring exclusively to the Roman Catholic Church. She claims that no one can interpret the Bible except bishops in communion with the pope of Rome.

What about when Sacred Scripture and Sacred Tradition conflict? The *Catechism of the Catholic Church* states:

> ...the Church, to whom the transmission and interpretation of Revelation is entrusted, does not derive her certainty about all revealed truths from the Holy Scriptures alone. Both Scripture and Tradition must be accepted and honored with equal sentiments of devotion and reverence.[127]

When it states, *"equal sentiments of devotion and reverence,"* one would assume that either source would suffice, but that is not the case within the teachings of Roman Catholicism. Sacred Tradition always overrides Sacred Scripture because the Sacred Traditions are often viewed as new revelations from God given through the pope. This is how the Roman Catholic Church has veered so far from the Word of God, with their papal created doctrines and dogmas. Because they teach that the reigning pope is the "Vicar of Christ," or Christ's representative on Earth, and that he is infallible when he speaks ex-cathedra, these doctrines and dogmas have been accepted as divine traditions which supersede the pure Word of God.

The Roman Catholic approved Bibles always include the *Apocrypha*, which consists of fourteen extra-biblical books. In the

---

[127] *Catechism of the Catholic Church,* Second Edition, 1997, paragraph 82

Greek language, the word "Apocrypha" means "hidden things".[128] The apocryphal books were written during a 400 year period when the prophets of God were silent. In the Bible, this time was between the Book of the prophet Malachi and the birth of Jesus, presented first in the Gospel of Matthew. None of the apocryphal writers claim Holy Spirit inspiration and their writings were never acknowledged as sacred Scripture by the Early Church. They were not allowed a place among the Scriptures during the first four centuries of the Early Church. For these reasons, the apocryphal books are merely valued as historical books of that time, but not inspired by the Holy Spirit.

Although the apocryphal writings were not accepted as canonical books of the Bible by the Early Church, many years later, with the help of the Jesuit Order during the Council of Trent in 1546, these writings were accepted as canons of Scripture within the Roman Catholic Church. A curse or "anathema" was pronounced upon anyone who would not accept all of the books of Jerome's Latin Vulgate, which was the approved Roman Catholic source.[129] The Roman Catholic Church bases some of their erroneous doctrines on passages taken from the Apocrypha, such as prayers to the dead and Purgatory, just to name two.

The *Catechism of the Catholic Church* has been mentioned as a reference countless times in this manuscript. It is nearly 1,000 pages in length and is the "go-to" manual for the beliefs of a Roman Catholic. The Catechism is used to teach religion at Roman Catholic Schools, as well as, to teach religion at the required Catechism classes.

---

[128] http://www.sacred-texts.com/chr/apo/index.htm
[129] *Why They Changed the Bible*, David W. Daniels, Chick Publications, 2014, page 170

Another significant manual for Roman Catholicism is the *Code of Canon Law*, which is a series of seven massive volumes full of rules, rules and more rules. Here is a description of the *Code of Canon Law* from the *Encyclopedia Britannica* online:[130]

> The second code, written in Latin, consists of 1,752 canons organized into 7 books. Books I and II define the positions and responsibilities of both the laity and the clergy; Book III deals with the promulgation of the church, including the subjects of teaching, preaching, and the church's relations with the media; Book IV contains guidelines for the administration of the sacraments, with the greatest emphasis on the sacrament of marriage; Book V concerns the church's handling of money, property, and other temporal goods; Book VI deals with sanctions, reducing the number of excommunicable actions from 37 to 7; and Book VII provides a structure for the establishment of church courts and the settlement of internal disputes.
>
> A chief element of the second code is the definition of the church as "the people of God" rather than as an institution.

Did you notice that the Roman Catholic Church refers to her faithful as **"the people of God?"** How can they adopt the name that God specifically gave the Jewish race? It is because Roman Catholicism teaches *"replacement theology,"* meaning that the Jews were replaced as God's chosen people by the members of the Roman Catholic Church. Paul clears this up in Romans 11: 1,

---

[130] https://www.britannica.com/topic/Code-of-Canon-Law

when he states, **"I say then, Has God cast away His people? God forbid. For I am also an Israelite, of the seed of Abraham, of the tribe of Benjamin."**

Because Roman Catholicism relies on the pope, a mortal man, to interpret God's desires for humanity, it has caused the creation of a myriad of unscriptural doctrines, traditions and commandments, which oppose the Word of God. Also, it is a little known fact that the Roman Catholic Church owns the copyrights to all of the newer Bible translations, which means that she can manipulate the Word of God and change God's pure words into the interpretations of man to suit her agenda.

MORMONISM

The Mormon Church accepts four "standard works" of Scripture: *The Book of Mormon, Doctrines and Covenants, Pearl of Great Price* and the Bible. They believe that the Bible text has been corrupted, so they only accept their own translation. This translation was written by Joseph Smith, who was not proficient in the Hebrew or Greek languages of which the Old and New Testaments were originally written. Let us look briefly at each significant book of the Mormon Church.

The Book of Mormon, published in 1830, was considered by Joseph Smith to be the *"most correct book on Earth,"* as well as, the *"most complete."* He claimed that he translated the Book of Mormon from the ancient writings of a prior civilization. Remember that Joseph Smith claims that the angel Moroni visited him on two occasions to point him to the ancient writings. Smith then says that he dug up the gold plates and transcribed the reformed Egyptian hieroglyphics using the seer stone found buried with the gold plates.

Doctrines and Covenants, originally called the *Book of Commandments,* was written three years after Joseph Smith wrote the Book of Mormon. This brings up the question: if The Book of Mormon was the *"most correct"* and the *"most complete"* book, why then did Joseph Smith feel the need to add to it with *Doctrines and Covenants*?

Pearl of Great Price is another "sacred" book of Mormonism, also written by Joseph Smith. He says that it was translated from various Egyptian artifacts. It includes Joseph Smith's own translations of the Book of Moses and the Gospel of Matthew, along with Mormon Articles of Faith. The Egyptian artifacts and old scrolls that Joseph Smith bought from a traveling show, along with some Egyptian mummies, were eventually proven to be remnants of a common Egyptian funeral text. What is so interesting is that Joseph Smith claimed that these were documents written by Abraham, 4,000 years earlier, and that he translated them using *"the gift and power of God."*[131]

Joseph Smith taught that every translation of the Bible up until his time was corrupted and so he set out to compile his own translation. Because he was neither a scholar, nor had any knowledge of the Hebrew or Greek languages, this would be a difficult task. Despite this fact, Smith made many thousands of changes to the King James Version Bible and passed it off as his own "inspired" translation. Not only did he fabricate a passage in the Book of Genesis predicting his own appearance, but he insisted that his translation of the Bible should be the only version that the Mormon Church should adopt.

---

[131] *World Religions and Cults 101,* Bruce Bickel and Stan Jantz, Harvest House Publishers, 2002, pages 97, 99

Call me crazy, but it seems very obvious that Joseph Smith was none other than a con-man. The fact that millions upon millions have bought into his unscriptural views is beyond comprehension. All of the books that Joseph Smith wrote were doctrines and commandments of men, which God forbids us to follow (Mark 7: 7, 8, 13).

JEHOVAH'S WITNESSES

When it comes to the Jehovah's Witnesses, they will claim that the Bible is their only authority and that they alone can interpret the Bible. However, Jehovah's Witnesses use their own proprietary version of the Bible, called the New World Translation of the Holy Scriptures.

The Jehovah's Witnesses hierarchy owns and operates The Watchtower Bible and Tract Society of Pennsylvania, which publishes all of their numerous materials. The publications include the New World Translation Bible, as well as, other important tracts used for door-to-door witnessing.

One of the most important publications of the Jehovah's Witnesses is *The Watchtower* magazine, which is used for instruction, as well as, field witnessing. The original magazine was written and published by Charles Taze Russell in 1881. *The Watchtower* magazine has the largest circulation than any magazine in the entire world, with distribution in 236 lands. It is printed in over 190 languages and each magazine run is over 42 million copies a month.

Another significant publication is *Awake*, which is also a doctrinal magazine published in over 80 languages and runs 42 million copies per month.[132] Other materials are also published and printed in Pennsylvania, including study aids, brochures and books.

Jehovah's Witnesses may claim that the Bible is their authority, but it is obvious that their New World Translation Bible has caused them to stray far from the pure Word of God. The fact that they do not see Jesus as God is a very serious issue, because if they disregard Jesus and His atoning work on the Cross, they clearly do not understand the story of the Bible. All of the hard work to publish and print their multi-millions of magazines each month to indoctrinate unsuspecting homeowners with their unscriptural cultic views is truly a waste of time, energy, paper and money.

SCIENTOLOGY

Let us look at what Scientology says when this question is posed on the Scientology website: *"Does Scientology have Scripture?"*

The written and recorded words of L. Ron Hubbard on the subject of Scientology collectively constitute the scripture of the religion. He set forth the Scientology theology and technologies in tens of millions

---

[132] http://www.jw.org/en/jehovahs-witnesses/activities/publishing/watchtowr-awake-magazine/

of words, including hundreds of books, scores of films and more than 3,000 recorded lectures.[133]

We have already briefly covered some of the more revolutionary writings of L. Ron Hubbard, such as *Dianetics: The Modern Science of Mental Health.* This is the book that put his name on the New York Times best sellers list for twenty-six consecutive weeks and sparked the interest in what became the religion of Scientology.

The interesting quote from the above statement is that Scientology outright states that L. Ron Hubbard wrote *"the scripture of the religion."* The word "Scripture" should be reserved solely for the Word of God, the Bible. It is blasphemy to label the writings of a man as "Scripture," especially when what L. Ron Hubbard taught was not even remotely close to the truth found in the Bible.

HINDUISM

The Hindu "holy" books originated when the Aryans assimilated into the culture of the Dravidians, who were occupying the Indus Valley River around 1500 B.C.[134] The Aryan religion was expressed in hymns, prayers and chants and was eventually compiled into the *Vedas.* Vedic literature was composed from

---

[133] https://www.scientology.org/faq/background-and-basic-principles/does-scientology-have-a-scripture.html
[134] *World Religions and Cults 101,* Bruce Bickel and Stan Jantz, Harvest House Publishers, 2002, pages 150-151

1400 to 400 B.C. and passed down for centuries until it was finally written down in the 14th century.

The Aryans spoke Sanskrit and they believed that the gods also spoke the same language, so the *Vedas* was written in Sanskrit. Vedas means "knowledge" and Hindus consider the Vedas to be supernaturally inspired. The early Vedic religion performed ritual sacrifices, but eventually the Vedas congregated more toward pantheism, meaning they believed that God is in every part of creation, *"God is all and all is God."*

The *Upanishad* was also mentioned in an earlier chapter. This subsequent set of Hindu writings gained popularity among the followers of the god, Brahma. It was because of the Upanishad that Hindu gurus were sought after for spiritual instruction. Vedanta, the school of thought which formed out of the Upanishad encouraged unity in diversity among Hindus.

Hinduism is paganism, comprising of the worship of multiple gods. God commanded us in Exodus 20: 3, **"Thou shall have no other gods before Me."** The Hindu "holy" book, the Vedas, originated out of the pagan Aryan religion, making it contrary to the Bible in its instruction for eternal salvation. While God portrays a simple plan of redemption in His Word, the Hindu religion complicates eternal salvation, making it almost unattainable.

BUDDHISM

In Buddhism, there are many Buddhist religious texts, which are divided into the categories of canonical and non-canonical. The canonical texts are called the *Sutras* in the Sanskrit language or *Suttas* in the Pali language. These are believed to be the actual words of the first Buddha, Siddhartha Gautama. The non-canonical texts are comprised of commentaries on canonical texts, discourses on dharma, as well as, collections of quotations and historical information from the religion of Buddhism.

Some of the Buddhists texts cross boundaries between canonical and non-canonical and some belong in both categories. The popular Zen Buddhism rejects Buddhist religious books altogether and considers them to be an ineffective path to enlightenment.

The *Tripitaka* is the earliest collection of Buddhist teachings and is considered canonical. Tripitaka means "three baskets," because the original text was written on long, narrow leaves, which were sewn at the edges, grouped into bunches and then stored in baskets. This same collection of texts is also referred to as the *Pali Canon*, after the language in which it was first written. It is a vast collection of writings, comprising up to fifty volumes and costing somewhere around $2,000 for a modern set.

The Tripitaka was handed down orally, then finally written down in the 3rd century B.C. According to Buddhist tradition, the contents of the Tripitaka were determined at the First Buddhist Council, shortly after the death of Buddha. As many as 500 of Buddha's disciples assembled, and at the direction of Mahakashypa, Buddha's successor, the teachings of Buddha were recited in full. They were then verified by others who had also been present and organized into the Tripitaka, although it was not written at the time of this council. The *Three Baskets* of the Tripitaka consist of:

- The *Vinaya Pitaka*, or "Discipline Basket," was recalled by a monk named Upali. This text is comprised of the rules and regulations for the monastic community, the *sangha*. It includes 227 rules for Buddhist monks, regulations for Buddhist nuns, and guidelines for the interaction between the sangha and the lay people. Most of these rules were derived from Buddha's code of conduct when dealing with situations in the community.

- The *Sutra Pitaka*, or "Discourse Basket," was recited by Ananda, Buddha's cousin and closest companion. It contains Buddha's teachings on doctrine and behavior, focusing especially on meditation techniques.
- The *Abhidharma Pitaka*, the "Higher Knowledge or Special Teachings Basket," was recited by Mahakashyapa, Buddha's immediate successor. It is comprised of a collection of miscellaneous writings, including songs, poetry, and stories of Buddha and his past lives. Its primary subjects are Buddhist philosophy and psychology. Also within the Abhidharma Pitaka is the *Dhammapada*, or *Dharmapada* in Sanskrit, a popular Buddhist text which consists of sayings of Buddha and simple discussions of Buddhist doctrine based on the Buddha's daily life.[135]

Another Buddhist non-canonical text is the *Tibetan Book of the Dead*. This Tibetan Buddhist text is the most well-known to the Western world. Tibetan Book of the Dead was written by a Tibetan monk and describes in great detail the stages of death from the Tibetan point of view. It chronicles the experiences and religious opportunities a person encounters at various stages of death and rebirth. This includes the moment when the person is dying, the moment of death, following with a forty-nine day interval period between death and rebirth, and then finally with rebirth.

In Tibet, Nepal, and Mongolia, a lama will often recite the Book of the Dead to a recently deceased person in order to help

---

[135] http://www.religionfacts.com/tripitaka

him understand his experiences, gain enlightenment and have a successful rebirth.

The Tibetan Book of the Dead is a product of the Nyingma School of Tibetan Buddhism. According to Nyingma tradition, the book was composed in the 8th century A.D. by Padmasambhava. He then concealed the book because he knew the world was not yet ready for its teachings. Concealed texts are called *terma*, meaning "treasure," and it is believed that they will not be discovered until the appointed time frame. The Tibetan Book of the Dead was rediscovered in the 14th century A.D. by Karma Lingpa, a monk of the Nyingma School.[136]

Buddhist books were written by mortal men. Even Buddha did not consider himself a god. While the writings are geared toward helping people live a better moral existence, it is encouraged outside of the understanding of the sin nature and the remedy for the problem of sin as given in the Word of God.

CONFUCIANISM

The core principles of Confucianism are compiled into nine books. Each of the nine books were individually written, however, they were categorized and assembled into two sets in the 12th century during the Sung Dynasty.

The first set is known as *The Five Classics* and was supposedly written even before the time of Confucius. The Five Classics consist of: *Shi Jing*, an anthology of 300 poems and songs; *Shu Jing*, a collection of historical documents attributed to the

---

[136] http://www.religionfacts.com/tibetan-book-dead

legendary and early leaders of China; *Li Ji,* a collection of writings relating to rituals; *Chun Qui,* an historical account of the Lu, the home region of Confucius; and *I Ching,* a collection of 64 hexagrams with specified meanings.

The second set are *The Four Books* containing the writings of Confucius and Mencius. These consist of: *Lun Yu,* often called the Analects and contains a record of the deeds and sayings of Confucius; *Chung Yung,* or "The Doctrine of the Mean"; *Ta Hsueh,* referred to as the Book of Great Learning; and *Meng Tzu,* the writings of Mencius, a contemporary of Confucius.

While most of these books were written by Confucius or his contemporaries, none were inspired by the Holy Spirit to point to God's redemption plan for mankind. Most of the books encourage a path of "moral evolution," meaning that man can progressively become a better person with his own self-efforts. None of this is scriptural and goes completely against what the Bible teaches in regard to man being born a sinner and needing to be "born again" by accepting God's sacrifice of Jesus Christ.

NEW AGE

One of the religious movements covered in the previous chapter was the New Age. As far as books and materials, the number of authors are way too many to thoroughly cover, but here are a select few of the most popular New Age authors today: Deepak Chopra (*You are the Universe,* among countless other books), Marianne Williamson (*Inspiring Teachings on A Course in Miracles* and many more), David Spangler (*Revelation: The Birth of a New Age* and others), Neale Donald Walsh (*Conversations with God* series), James Redfield (*The Celestine Prophecy* series) and Rhonda Byrne (*The Secret* series). Many of these authors will admit to being inspired by their "spirit guides" or an "inner voice" to write their materials.

We already covered Helena Blavatsky's and Alice Bailey's inspiration, but one more significant author of the New Age worth mentioning is Helen Schucman. She wrote *A Course in Miracles* over a seven year period, beginning in 1965, as an "inner voice" dictated the material to her. Here is a quote from the highly celebrated New Age book, *A Course in Miracles*:

> ...do not make the pathetic error of clinging to the old rugged cross... the journey to the cross should be the last useless journey... the recognition of God is the recognition of yourself... there is no sin, it has no consequence... Christ takes many forms with different names until their oneness can be recognized. [137]

Because *A Course in Miracles* is considered to be a manual for the New Age religion, it is clear that the New Age is completely contradictory to the teachings of the Bible. This goes for all of the other writers and their books, which promote Eastern mysticism and discovering the "god within," through meditation and enlightenment. The lie of the Serpent of Genesis is so evident within the New Age, but those who refuse to read the Word of God will remain in the dark.

---

[137] *Deceived on Purpose,* Warren Smith, Mountain Stream Press, California, 2004, pages 88-89

LUCIFERIANSIM & SATANISM

The Book of Lucifer is one of the popular writings for Luciferians. It is said to have been originally written in human blood upon the parchment of human skin. The oldest known form of The Book of Lucifer is the ancient vulgar of pagan Rome from about the 4th century A.D. The introduction to this book states:

> You will find the 4th century Latin preceding the English translations in this remarkable work throughout all of its chapters.

> Beware of The Curse of Lucifer that precedes the chapters of this manuscript.

> For you will indeed suffer the plagues contained within The Book of Lucifer if you add even one word to it![138]

Other books that are highly recommended for one who would delve in Luciferianism are all books by Michael W. Ford. Some titles for beginners include: *Adversarial Light – Magick of the Nephilim; Sebitti- Mesopotamian Magick & Demonology; Beginning Luciferian Magick; Geotia of Shadows: Luciferian Ceremonial Sorcery and Magick; Bible of the Adversary and NECROMINON - Egyptian Sethanic Magick.*[139]

---

[138] http://netaimstuff.tripod.com/sitebuildercontent/sitebuilderfiles/lucifer.pdf
[139] https://www.luciferianapotheca.com/blogs/news/4104662-what-books-do-i-start-with-for-studying-luciferianism

There are different sects of Satanism, such as Theistic Satanism and LaVeyan Satanism, as well as others, but there does not seem to be one official holy or sacred book of the religion of Satanism. Each sect has their own rituals and books.

LaVeyan Satanism, which began in 1966, was founded by Anton LaVey. He is also the founder of the Church of Satan and the author of the *Satanic Bible* and *Satanic Rituals*. Needless to say, the *Satanic Bible* is the upside down gospel of the true Bible inspired by the Holy Spirit. Not at all ironic, one of the many symbols of Satanism is Jesus crucified on an upside down cross.

AGNOSTICISM & ATHEISM

Since Agnosticism and Atheism are not true religions per se, neither has a sacred text. Because the term "sacred" implies "handed down by a god," both belief systems would not consider any book to be sacred, because they would be attributing it to a God in whom they do not believe. Of course, there are countless books circulating which have been written by Atheists and Agnostics, but no particular "holy" or "sacred" texts.

The goal of this chapter was to acknowledge the divine inspiration of the Holy Spirit in the writing of the Bible, which is the literal Word of God. None of the other books described in this chapter point to God's simple plan of salvation. The other books were written by men and give a path to redemption or no afterlife at all, that does not line up with God's Word. No other book we reviewed has the element of prophecy and the fulfillment of those prophecies, which prove that the omniscient God is the author. But regrettably, we are a society swimming in intellect and knowledge, but drowning in obliviousness and willful ignorance.

Chapter Fifteen

OIL & WATER

Likely, we've all heard the expression, *"oil and water cannot mix."* This chapter is about the opposite spectrums of both "law and grace" and "the flesh and the Spirit," which are much like oil and water. One always prevails above the other and because they war against one another, neither of these two spectrums can function at the same given time.

God loves us enough to extend His grace to each and every one of us, but we can only receive His free gift of grace if we first let go of "law." Here is a quick analogy to help you to better understand how law and grace cannot operate simultaneously. Your hands are full of several volumes of large, heavy books, and all the while, God is trying to hand you a gift that He is anxious for you to receive. There is no way that you can squeeze anything else into your hands, so, in order to receive God's gift, you must first set down all of the books.

That gift, of course, represents the grace of God, which was extended to us by what Jesus accomplished when He died on the Cross for the sins of mankind. The books represent all of the man-made laws and religious regulations that are forced on us, as well as, those that we place upon ourselves in an attempt to please God. Now, just imagine how free you would feel without the burden of those heavy books! That is how you can feel every single day when you let go of "law," accept God's gift of grace, which then allows you to walk in the Spirit and not after the flesh.

Romans 8: 1-2 explains this position well, when Paul says, **"There is therefore now no condemnation to them which are** in Christ Jesus, who walk not after the flesh, but after the Spirit. For the law of the Spirit of life in Christ Jesus has made me free from the law of sin and death." Let us take a look at what these two laws represent.

The **"law of the Spirit of life in Christ Jesus"** and **"the law of sin and death"** are the two most powerful laws in the entire Universe. The **"law of sin and death"** is what we received at birth, as descendants of Adam's fallen race. But the **"law of the Spirit of life in Christ Jesus"** has the ability reverse **"the law of sin and death."** This can only happen when we place our faith in Jesus' finished work on the Cross, which allows the Holy Spirit to help us walk in victory.

The Scripture in Romans Chapter 8 goes on to give an excellent comparison of "the law", "the flesh" and "the Spirit." Paul states, **"For what the law could not do, in that it was weak through the flesh, God sending his own Son in the likeness of sinful flesh** (the incarnation)**, and for sin, condemned sin in the flesh. That the righteousness of the law** (Law of Moses) **might be fulfilled in us, who walk not after the flesh but after the Spirit. For they that are after the flesh do mind the things of the flesh; but they that are after the Spirit the things of the Spirit. For to be carnally minded is death, but to be spiritually minded is life and peace. Because the carnal mind is at enmity against God: for it is not subject to the law of God, neither indeed can be. So then they that are in the flesh cannot please God... For as many as are led by the Spirit of God, they are the sons of God** (Romans 8: 3-8, 14) (My notes in parentheses)**."**

When God looks at mankind, He sees only two separate categories: the redeemed and the unredeemed. We have already mentioned that our acceptance into Heaven *will not* be likened to a scale that weighs our good and evil deeds against one another. Besides, we would never be "good enough" anyway because James 2: 10 says, **"For whosoever shall keep the whole Law, and yet** offend in one point, he is guilty of all." We are not expected to be perfect, but *we are expected to put our faith in the one who was and is perfect, Jesus Christ!*

The **"whole Law"** that James is referring to here is the Mosaic Law, which consisted of 613 laws and was issued to the Israelites in order to define "sin." But, this Law was only needed until the Redeemer came to free them from sin. Galatians 3: 19 says, **"Wherefore then serves the Law? It was added because of transgressions, til the Seed** (Jesus) **should come to whom the Promise was made...** (My notes in parentheses)" The words, **"...til the Seed should come..."** reveals that the Law of Moses was temporary and would be completely fulfilled once the promised Redeemer came. Jesus fulfilled the Law of Moses in totality by keeping the Law perfectly; something that no other earthly person had been able to do.

Jesus said in Matthew 5: 17, **"Think not that I come to destroy the Law or the Prophets: I am not some to destroy, but to fulfill."** Then, Galatians 3: 23-25 says, **"But before faith came, we were kept under the Law, shut up unto the faith which should afterwards be revealed. Wherefore the Law was our schoolmaster to bring us unto Christ, that we might be justified by faith. But after that faith is come, we are no longer under a schoolmaster."** This is showing that *Jesus was the end of the Law and the beginning of grace.*

Today, we no longer have to keep the Mosaic Law, but religion of every kind is famous for putting people under "law," or man-inspired rules and regulations, which an individual must follow to be accepted into their fold or to make it to Heaven upon death. Other sources of "law," are the rules and regulations we place upon ourselves in an attempt to impress God with our holiness and righteousness. Is God impressed?

Galatians 2: 21 reveals the answer to that question when it states, **"I do not frustrate the grace of God: for if righteousness** come by the Law, then Christ is dead in vain." Also, Romans 6: 14 says, **"For sin shall not have dominion over you: for you are not under the Law, but under grace."** Then Romans 10: 4 really drives home the point when Paul says, **"For Christ is the end of the Law for righteousness to everyone who believes."**

The good news is that because Jesus fulfilled the Mosaic Law completely, we can also be law keepers and stay in a right standing relationship with God the Father. That may sound impossible when we look again at James 2:10 which says, **"For whosoever shall keep the whole Law, and yet offend in one point, he is guilty of all."** With our inherited sin nature, how can we manage to keep the whole Law and never stumble?

Would you believe that God can look at us as never having sinned and as perfect keepers of His Law simply by placing our faith in Jesus Christ and what He accomplished on the Cross when He defeated sin, death and Satan? Remember, Jesus kept the Law perfectly, never sinning even once. 2 Corinthians 5: 21 says, **"For He** (God) **has made Him** (Jesus) **to be sin** (a sin- offering) **for us, who knew no sin that we might be made the righteousness of God in Him** (My notes in parentheses)."

When Jesus was buried in the tomb, the sins of every believer were buried along with Him. And when God raised Jesus from the dead three days later, He raised every believer into a new creation with every sin remaining in that tomb! Here is the proof in Romans 6: 3-4, where it states **"Know you not, that so many of us as were baptized into Jesus Christ were baptized into his death? Therefore we are buried with him by baptism into death: that like as Christ was raised up from the dead by the glory of the Father, even so we also should walk in newness of life."**

Now that we have dealt with the opposite continuum of law and grace, let us look at the difference between "walking after the flesh" and "walking after the Spirit." Walking after the flesh constitutes looking to our own abilities, strengths or following man-made laws to earn something from God, whether it be for salvation or sanctification.[140] Walking after the flesh is dependence on "self" to earn God's grace. Consequently, walking after the Spirit is when we place our faith in the finished work of Jesus on the Cross and believe that He paid for everything that we need, including our salvation, as well as, our sanctification. Walking after the Spirit is when we understand that there is nothing that we can do to earn anything from God, outside of our faith in what Jesus has already accomplished.

God demonstrated the separation of flesh for the child of God by the command that all male Jews were to be circumcised as a fulfillment of God's covenant with Abraham (Genesis 17: 10-13). Circumcision required a literal removal of the "flesh," via the male foreskin and represented the putting away of the filth of the flesh. It also represented the shedding of blood, which was later fulfilled by Jesus on the Cross.

Operating in the flesh can have terrible consequences, as Abraham and Sarah regrettably discovered. Their carnally minded plans have affected the entire world. Let me explain. God had promised Abraham on many occasions that his descendants would be more than the **"stars of the heaven"** and more than the **"sand upon the sea"** (Genesis 22: 17). The problem was that according to Abraham and Sarah, God was taking way too long to fulfill His promise. As a result of their impatience, they devised a plan, in their own flesh, to have Abraham go into Sarah's handmaid, Hagar, to conceive a child.

Abraham and Sarah's plan worked and Hagar conceived Ishmael, who became the father of the Arab race. After the

---

[140] Sanctification: to live holy for God and be set apart for His purpose alone.

pregnant Hagar flees from camp, because Sarah deals harshly with her, God sends an Angel of the Lord to speak with her. The Angel says in Genesis 16: 10, **"... I will multiply your seed exceedingly, that it shall not be numbered for multitude."** Then in Genesis 16: 12, the Angel of the Lord describes Ishmael saying, **"And he will be a wild man; his hand will be against every man, and every man's hand against him; and he shall dwell in the presence of all his brethren."** This Scripture very well depicts the Arab population over the centuries, as well as, present day.

One of the major reasons for the incessant fighting in Israel is that God promised this land to His chosen people through the seed of Abraham, Isaac and Jacob. In the Bible, Israel was originally called Canaan, which was **"the land flowing with milk and honey."** The Arabs believe that this land was promised to them through Ishmael, because he was born to Abraham first. In their opinion, Ishmael owned the birthright, thereby laying claim to the land which God had promised to Abraham. This is an understandable argument, but God is referred to as **"the God of Abraham, Isaac and Jacob"** sixteen times in the Bible. The Arabs have been warring with the Jews for thousands of years over the land of Israel and over the mere existence the Jewish race.

As we can see, operating in the flesh effects not only the individual, but others, as well. God did eventually fulfill His promise to Abraham and Sarah and she conceived Isaac in her old age. What is the moral of the story? Wait on God and let His Holy Spirit guide you, instead of walking after the flesh and wrecking all of His plans.

Can a believer in Jesus Christ operate in the flesh and be under law? Most certainly! Unfortunately, when a person is saved, he does not always understand how to walk with God in victory. Paul tells the Galatian Church in Galatians 3: 3, **"O foolish Galatians! Who has bewitched you! Having begun in the Spirit, are you now being made perfect by the flesh?"** He was telling the Galatian Church that they began correctly in their walk by relying on the Spirit of God, but now they are attempting to sanctify themselves through works of the flesh.

Paul tells them in Galatians 2: 16, **"Knowing that man is not justified by the works of the law, but by the faith of Jesus Christ, even we have believed in Jesus Christ, that we might be justified by the faith of Christ, and not by the works of the law: for by the works of the law shall no flesh be justified."**

This is the trap that many Christians fall into after their initial salvation experience. Not understanding the finished work of Jesus on the Cross, they try to earn God's grace through law and works of the flesh. Here is an example: *"I am going to read three Chapters a day in my Bible, pray for one hour a day and give money to the poor."* Despite the fact that all of these things are admirable, this person has just put himself under law. How?

We have already briefly discussed our motives toward God. Does this person want to do these things to impress God or to earn favor from God? If the answer is yes, then performing these works is useless. Now, let us look at this in a different way. If the same person decides to read his Bible to learn more about God and the things of God; if he prays because he wants to worship God, thank God and pray for others; and if he gives to the poor by not just giving of material things, but also sharing the Gospel, then all of these things are pleasing to God. The difference is that the person is walking in the Spirit and not after the flesh, which Paul stated earlier in Romans 8: 8, **"cannot please God."**

The Bible explains it time and time again that law and grace cannot mix and that Jesus Christ was the end of the Law for those who will place their faith in His once and for all sacrifice. The Word of God also tells us in Galatians 5: 16-17, **"This I say then, walk in the Spirit, and you shall not fulfill the lust of the flesh. For the flesh lusts against the Spirit, and the Spirit against the flesh; and these are contrary the one to the other..."**

Man always tries to complicate God's simple plan of salvation by adding their own laws, rules, sacraments and regulations. Most of the time, these are unattainable goals so that the people of different religions continue daily on the hamster wheel of law, trying desperately to please God. All God wants us to do is rest in what Jesus has already done, accept the grace He afforded us and let the Holy Spirit guide us to live a life that is pleasing to God. Why complicate something that God has made so simple?

Chapter Sixteen

A THIEF & A ROBBER

In 1969, Paul Anka wrote a song, which was recorded by Frank Sinatra called, *"My Way."* Here are the opening and closing lyrics of that song:

> And now, the end is near
> And so I face the final curtain
> My friend, I'll say it clear
> I'll state my case, of which I'm certain
>
> For what is a man, what has he got
> If not himself, then he has naught
> To say the things he truly feels
> And not the words of one who kneels
> The record shows I took the blows
> And did it my way

I think that a lot of people can relate to these lyrics because most of us want to do things *our own way*. We were taught in school to *"be independent,"* which can be confusing when a person is born again and must learn to yield himself to God and rely on the help of the Holy Spirit. And it is especially difficult for someone who has not yet been saved to see that his own way can often lead to a downward spiral into an eternal separation from God.

In this chapter, we will look into what the Bible reveals concerning the various paths that people take in an effort to reach

Heaven. Earlier we quoted Matthew 7: 13-14, where Jesus says, **"Enter you in at the strait gate: for wide is the gate, and broad is the way, that leads to destruction, and many there be which go in thereat: Because strait is the gate, and narrow is the way, which leads unto life, and few there be that find it."**

Jesus plainly tells us that there is a strait gate and a narrow way which leads unto eternal life, or Heaven. In the beginning of the Scripture, He specifically commands us to **"Enter you in at the strait gate."** Jesus also says that only a few will discover this narrow way. If it does not seem fair that only a few will find the correct way, please know that it is not because God will only allow a select few into Heaven. On the contrary, it is because man has free will and most will choose to reject God's simple way and choose their own path. Remember that God is **"not willing that *any* should perish, but that *all* should come to repentance** (2 Peter 3: 9) (My italics).**"**

On the other hand, Jesus warns us that many will enter the wide gate and the broad way, which leads to **"destruction."** *Thayer's Greek Lexicon* defines the word "destruction" used in this Scripture reference as: *"the destruction which consists of the loss of eternal life; eternal misery; perdition."*[141] These are pretty strong words! Jesus is compelling us to avoid the loss of eternal life and a life of eternal misery by entering in at the strait and narrow gate. Where can we find the gate of which Jesus speaks?

The first mention of **"the gate"** is in Exodus 27: 14 and 16. This portion of Scripture encompassed the period of time when God was delivering to Moses the precise instructions for building the Tabernacle of the Congregation. If you will remember, the entire structure of the Tabernacle represented the

---

[141] https://www.blueletterbible.org/lang/lexicon/lexicon.cfm?Strongs=G684&t=KJV

coming Redeemer, Jesus Christ, in every single detail. Please refer back to pages 49-50 of this book for a quick review if needed.

"The Gate" was the *one and only way* into the Tabernacle of the Congregation and was also known as **"the Way."** Jesus referred to Himself as **"the way, the truth and the life"** and said that **"no man comes to the Father but by Me** (John 14: 6)."

Jesus also said in John 10: 9, **"I am the Door: by Me if any man enter in, he shall be saved."** And one of the most compelling Scriptures is found in John 10: 1, where Jesus warns, **"Verily, verily, I say unto you, He who enters not by the door into the sheepfold, but climbs up *some other way,* the same is *a thief and a robber*** (My italics)."

Who falls into the category of **"a thief and a robber,"** and what can we do to avoid falling victim to this snare? Anyone who accepts another way to be saved, other than through Jesus' death on the Cross is **"a thief and a robber."** This includes all of the many religions, cults and philosophies that we have covered thus far in this book. Let us briefly look at each one again.

Judaism refuses to accept that Jesus Christ was indeed the Messiah sent by God 2,000 years ago. If the religious Jews could have their way, the Temple would still be standing today, so that they could continue to offer animal sacrifices. Instead of concentrating on *who* the animal sacrifices represented and understanding that it was a type and shadow of the Redeemer to come, the Jews got caught up in the religious ceremony of it and missed the very last **"Lamb of God who takes away the sin of the world** (John 1: 29)."

During the reign of the Antichrist, whom the Jews will believe to be their long-awaited Messiah, the temple will be rebuilt and the sacrifices will be offered again for a short time. Unfortunately, the Jewish object of faith is in the religious ceremony and not in Jesus Christ, the Saviour of the world. This makes the religion of Judaism a **"thief and a robber."**

What about Islam? This religion teaches that Jesus is merely a prophet and that He is not the Son of God. A Muslim's salvation is only made possible by appeasing Allah with the Five Pillars of Islam. Muslims must work diligently for redemption because they will find no rest in the finished work of Jesus. This path of salvation is indicative of **"a thief and a robber."**

The Roman Catholic Church believes that salvation is only through membership into her ecclesiastical organization and that one must take part in her sacramental system in order to go to Heaven. But, as previously stated, no one can ever be certain of salvation and it is a *"sin of presumption"* to claim that one has any assurance of Heaven. They teach that sins must be confessed to a priest and that even after death, one must purge past sins in the painful fires of Purgatory. Their "Jesus" offers himself at each Mass in the form of a wafer of bread, to be crucified again and again for the remission of sins. All of this completely nullifies Jesus' finished work on the Cross, because the individual is responsible for earning salvation. This route constitutes **"a thief and a robber."**

Mormonism teaches that Jesus and Lucifer were brothers, the result of Father God procreating with Mother God via intercourse. The Bible says nothing of the sort. Mormons base their salvation on good works and being submissive to the "gospel" of the Mormon Church. Their "gospel" is a far cry from the good news of the Bible and includes preexistence, the potential to become a god and a planet all of their own someday, where they will have multitudes of spirit children. Mormonism may claim to be "Christian," but the beliefs and teachings of the Mormon Church make it a prime example of **"a thief and a robber."**

Jehovah's Witnesses also deny that Jesus is the Son of God and spend all of their energy at Kingdom Hall meetings and door-to-door witnessing, in an attempt to add more people to their cult. They teach that only 144,000 people will go to Heaven and that the rest of the Jehovah's Witnesses will live on a purified Earth.

The man-made restrictions placed upon Jehovah's Witnesses puts them under law, thereby forfeiting the grace that God offers them through the blood of Jesus Christ. Because they do not see Jesus' death on the Cross as anything significant, they have completely missed the source of salvation making them another group under the heading of **"a thief and a robber."**

Scientologists do not even mention the **"Name above all names,"** Jesus, in their teachings. Why would they, when their founder believes that we possess the internal power to save ourselves. Remember the introduction to Scientology on their official website? It stated, *"Scientology further holds man to be basically good, and that his spiritual salvation depends on himself, his fellows and his attainment of brotherhood with the universe... Scientology is not a dogmatic religion in which one is asked to accept anything on faith alone."*

The statement concerning *"faith alone"* is a stab at true Christianity, which teaches that faith alone in the finished work of Jesus Christ is the source of salvation. This religion blatantly rebukes God's free gift of salvation and this makes Scientology **"a thief and a robber."**

In Hindu teachings and beliefs, Jesus is absolutely non-existent. The salvation of a Hindu is dependent upon the wheel of karma, which weighs good works against bad actions. Their hope is to be reincarnated into someone of a higher caste after death and eventually be liberated from the birth-death cycle all together once they become one with the Universe. Through works and worshipping of multiple gods, the Hindu's faith is solely on his own performance. Because they have taken Jesus completely out of the equation, Hinduism's path to redemption qualifies it to be **"a thief and a robber."**

The Buddhist way of thought is that one can achieve *nirvana*, or freedom from the reincarnation cycle and end the suffering of the present life by following the teachings of Buddha.

This is accomplished through works by following Buddha's Four Noble Truths, his Eightfold Path, his Three Jewels and also, by meditating and practicing yoga. Overall, Buddhism teaches that one must reject the present world and morally evolve through the guidelines mentioned above. There is no promise of "salvation," but instead, Buddhism teaches that eventually one will reach nirvana and that the life of the person is extinguished forever. Not only does Buddhism ignore Jesus Christ, but the promise of nirvana is solely based on the performance of the individual. This makes the religion of Buddhism **"a thief and a robber."**

Confucianism is all about an individual's good moral behavior paralleling with their lifetime relationships. If you will remember, there is no God or Jesus at all in Confucianism. The focus is a good life for the present, because there is no ultimate eternal salvation or afterlife. The person who practices Confucianism has to depend on their own personal ability to live a morally good life by the works of the flesh. With its rejection of everything the Bible teaches, Confucianism certainly falls into the category of **"a thief and a robber."**

The New Age religion is nothing new, but a form a worship of the "serpent of Genesis," as well as, worship of "self." This belief system really began in the Garden of Eden at the Fall of Man. I would say that the true founder of the New Age religion is Lucifer and his first converts were Adam and Eve, who rejected God's divine protection for an opportunity to be like gods themselves. Because the New Age teaches that one can become a god, the lie of the serpent has deeply penetrated their belief system. The New Age is the complete antithesis of the Bible and God's plan of salvation, making it **"a thief and a robber."**

It goes without saying that Luciferianism and Satanism most definitely conflict with God's plan of salvation as given to us in the Bible. Within the two, God is seen as an oppressive and controlling villain, while Lucifer is viewed as an outright hero and

Satan is seen as the revelation of personal freedom and rebellion against the establishment of God's kingdom.

Both believe that man can become enlightened and discover his own divinity, making him equal to god. Sadly, they have believed the lie of the serpent in the Garden of Eden and will pay dearly in eternity for their delusion. 2 Thessalonians 2: 10-12 states, **"And with all deceivableness of unrighteousness in them who perish;** *because they received not the love of the truth, that they might be saved.* **And for this cause** *God shall send them strong delusion, that they shall believe a lie.* **That they all might be damned who believed not the truth, but had pleasure in unrighteousness** (My italics)." I think that it is safe to say that both Luciferianism and Satanism most certainly can be labeled as **"a thief and a robber."**

Lastly, when it comes to Agnosticism and Atheism, there is no belief in God, Jesus, salvation, an afterlife or anything that has to do with eternity. The Bible is completely rejected and traded for man's interpretation of creation and humanity's role in that creation. Because there is no path or direction, they do not promote a false way of salvation, but simply cast-off any chance of eternity, whether in Heaven or in Hell. Agnostics and Atheists have created their own reality outside of the Word of God, and therefore their apathetic views earn them the title of **"a thief and a robber,"** simply because they are leading millions down the wrong path to the **"broad"** and **"wide"** gate, which leads to perdition.

Something we have already dealt with in this book is the mind-set that there are many paths to Heaven and that once we die, we will go directly to Heaven. Let's see what Jesus says concerning this in Matthew 7: 21, where He stated, **"Not everyone who says unto Me, Lord, Lord, shall enter into the Kingdom of Heaven; but he who does the will of My Father which is in Heaven."** When He says, **"the will of My Father,"**

Jesus is referring to accepting the grace, which God has freely given us, through Jesus' death on the Cross.

Earlier we asked the question of how to avoid becoming **"a thief and a robber,"** so that we can spend eternity in Heaven. The only way is if we follow the command given in John 3: 3, when Jesus said to Nicodemus, a religious leader of Israel, **"Verily, Verily, I say unto you, except a man be born again, he cannot see the Kingdom of God."** The **"Kingdom of God,"** mentioned here is referring to Heaven, and it is our reward for accepting God's way and not our own. It is a complete denial of our own flesh and requires faith in the fact that Jesus paid our sin debt at Calvary.

Nicodemus was confused by this statement and asked Jesus in John 3: 4, **"How can a man be born when he is old? Can he enter a second time into his mother's womb, and be born?"** Jesus responded by saying, **"Verily, verily, I say unto you, except a man be born of water and of the Spirit, he cannot enter into the Kingdom of God** (John 3: 5)."

Our initial birth of water, from our mother's womb, was contaminated with the sin nature because of the Fall of Man. Jesus said that we must be **"born again"** of the Spirit because the curse of Adam's fall must be broken. When we admit that we were born with the sin nature and that Jesus is the only one who can save us, we become **"partakers of the divine nature** (2 Peter 2: 4)." This divine nature is afforded to us only by Jesus's death on the Cross, which defeated Satan, who brought sin and death into this world in the first place. This spiritual rebirth is *mandatory* for any human being who desires to enter the Kingdom of God. No ifs, and or buts about it!

Chapter Seventeen

THE MOST GRIEVOUS SIN

Is it enough to simply believe that Jesus existed? Well, the Bible says in James 2:19, **"You believe that there is one God...the Devils also believe, and tremble."** Satan believes that Jesus exists, however, Revelation 20:10 foretells that he will spend his eternity in the Lake of Fire. It takes more than believing in the mere existence of Jesus Christ to attain eternal life in Heaven.

So far, the Scriptures have proven that God's only path to eternal life in Heaven is contingent upon our *acceptance* of His sacrifice on our behalf. This sacrifice being the only begotten Son of God, Jesus Christ. John 3: 16, quoted earlier, plainly states, **"For God so loved the world, that He gave His only begotten Son, that whosoever believes in Him, should not perish but have everlasting life."** Satan's ultimate goal is to divert God's plan by encouraging *man to create his own way to eternal life* and this is the most damnable sin in the eyes of God.

Yes, you read that correctly, *the most grievous sin is the rejection of Jesus Christ as the source of eternal salvation.* That is the problem with religion and even with those who cast off all forms of religion and simply go their own way in life, hoping that they were good enough for Heaven once they die. We already covered that 1 Peter 1: 18-19 says, **"Forasmuch as you know that you were not redeemed with corruptible things, as silver and gold, from your vain conversation received by tradition from your fathers; But with the precious blood of Christ, as of a Lamb without blemish and without spot..."** We cannot buy or earn our salvation, it only comes through the blood that Jesus shed for us on the Cross.

Participating in a religion may cause a person to feel a sense of spiritual accomplishment, but to God, these man-made religions propagate spiritual adultery and are an abomination. We are warned numerous times in the Word of God to abstain from adultery. However, it is clear in that the sin of adultery is referring to more than the sinful act of infidelity among married couples. Adultery also references a spiritual wandering of the heart from our **"first love** (Revelation 2: 4),**"** who is always to be Jesus Christ. Ezekiel 23: 37 says, **"... they have committed adultery, and blood is in their hands, and with their idols, they have committed adultery."**

2 Timothy 3: 1-7 sums up the condition of most men in the last days. It says, **"This know also, that in the last days perilous times shall come. For men shall be lovers of their own selves, covetous, boasters, proud, blasphemers, disobedient to parents, unthankful, unholy, without natural affection, trucebreakers, false accusers, incontinent, fierce, despisers of those who are good, traitors, heady, high-minded, lovers of pleasures more than lovers of God; Having a form of godliness, but denying the power thereof...Ever learning, and never able to come to the knowledge of truth: men of corrupt minds, reprobate concerning the Faith."** Sadly, this is a perfect description of humanity today.

As a result of the Bible and prayer being taken out of public schools, the world we live in continues to spiral into utter mayhem. 2 Timothy 3: 13 explains: **"But evil men and seducers shall wax worse and worse, deceiving and being deceived."** Compile this with man-made religion taking the place of Biblical truth and it is a recipe for moral decay, destruction and death. Man has no victory outside of the Cross of Jesus Christ and that is why the world is growing worse and worse.

Even so-called Christian churches have fallen victim to the

"Seeker-Sensitive Church" model being propagated by many well-known "CEO pastors" today. This includes the Emerging Church Movement, the Purpose Driven Church Movement, as well as any individual church pastor who preaches self-help and Humanistic Psychology instead of the true Gospel of Jesus Christ. The result is that churches are large in number, but the people who fill the seats are living in sin and defeat because they do not understand God's prescribed order of victory. To refresh the reader, our victory comes through Jesus Christ as the object of our faith, the Cross as the means by which Jesus defeated sin, death, Satan and Hell and when we continually place our faith in Jesus' sacrifice, the Holy Spirit can lead us in victory, as we learn to yield our lives to the will of God.

The religions that do acknowledge Jesus, unfortunately have the wrong view of who He is and His true purpose. Remember, Paul warned us in 2 Corinthians 11: 3-4, saying, **"But I fear, lest by any means, as the serpent beguiled Eve through his subtlety, so your minds should be corrupted from the simplicity that is in Christ. For if he who comes preaching another Jesus, whom we have not preached, or *if* you receive another spirit which you have not received, or another gospel, which you have not accepted, you might well bear with him."**

The work of Jesus is a finished work. Mark 16: 19 records Jesus' ascension into Heaven saying, **"So then after the Lord had spoken unto them, He was received into Heaven, and sat on the right hand of the Father."** And Hebrews 1: 3 states, **"...when He had by Himself purged our sins, sat down on the right hand of the Majesty on High."** Both of these Scriptures signify a completed work and show that Jesus is sitting, or resting, on the right hand of God the Father in Heaven. Jesus fulfilled the Sabbath rest, as well as, the need for animal sacrifices to cover sin. Jesus even cried, **"It is finished"** in John 19: 30, just moments before He **"gave up the ghost."**

Here are some Scriptures proving that Jesus' sacrifice of Himself on the Cross for the sins of humanity was a once and for all finished work and never needs repeating. Hebrews 10: 11 says, **"And every Priest stands daily ministering and offering oftentimes the same sacrifices, which can never take away sins."** Remember that the **"blood of bulls and goats"** was a substitute for the real **"Lamb of God,"** and could only cover sin. But, the blood of Jesus could take sin away forever.

Remember that Hebrews 9: 24-26 says, **"For Christ is not entered into the Holy Places made with hands...but to Heaven itself, now to appear in the presence of God for us: Nor yet that He should offer Himself often, as the High Priest enters into the Holy Place every year with the blood of others; For then must He often have suffered since the foundation of the world: but now once in the end of the world has He appeared to put away sin by the sacrifice of Himself."** This is speaking of the blood of the sacrificial animals, used to represent the blood that Jesus would shed for us and then shows that Jesus **"put away sin"** with His death on the Cross.

Hebrews 10:10 says, **"... we are sanctified through the Offering of the Body of Jesus Christ once for all."** The phrase, **"once for all"** means that the sacrifice never needs repeating.

Moses, a true servant of God, was not allowed to enter the Promised Land of Canaan because of disobeying God's command concerning the striking of the **"Rock."** In Exodus 17: 6, God told Moses, **"Behold, I will stand before you there upon the Rock of Horeb, and you shall smite the Rock, and there shall come water out of it, that the people may drink. And Moses did so in the site of the Elders of Israel."**

Let's set the stage for what is taking place here. Moses has been used by God to deliver the Israelites out of Pharaoh's control and then God leads them into the wilderness, where there is no food or water. God provides sustenance for them with manna from Heaven to eat and then instructs Moses to strike the **"Rock"** with his rod so that water will spring forth to quench the thirst of the people. **"That Rock was Christ,"** as 1 Corinthians 10: 4 plainly states and the striking of the Rock with the rod represented Jesus' crucifixion.

Now, let us fast forward to Numbers Chapter 20, where God tells Moses to **"speak unto the Rock"** and **"you shall bring forth them water out of the Rock** (Numbers 20: 7-10)."** Regrettably, instead of speaking to the Rock, Numbers 20: 11 says, **"And Moses lifted up his hand, and with the rod he smote the Rock twice..."** The striking of the Rock a second time is symbolic of crucifying Jesus Christ again, meaning that His sacrifice was somehow insufficient and needed to be repeated.

God allowed the people to drink, but then He says to Moses in Numbers 20: 12, **"...Because you believed Me not, to sanctify Me in the eyes of the Children of Israel, therefore you shall not bring this congregation into the land which I have given to them."** This punishment does not abrogate the fact that Moses was used of God greatly, but the chastisement was harsh because the sin of Moses was serious. Moses would die atop Mount Nebo before he had an opportunity to stand on the threshold of Canaan. Despite the fact that Moses invested so much into leading the Children of God to the Promised Land, it would be Joshua who would complete the mission.

The last topic we will cover in this chapter includes the fact that many people want to acknowledge Jesus as their Saviour, but they do not want Him as the Lord of their life. What is the difference? Jesus saving us from our sins sounds wonderful because everyone wants to be unburdened from the constraint of sin. Thankfully, Jesus will do that for us, but if we stop short there, very likely we will eventually walk away from our faith.

Many believe that once a person is saved, then no matter what he does and no matter how hellacious he lives, that he is bound for Heaven upon death. They often quote the Scripture in John 10: 29, which says, **"...and no man is able to pluck them out of my Father's hand."** *The truth is that God will never turn His back on us, but we can certainly choose to walk away from the redemption He has given us.*

Man has free will and sometimes he chooses to exercise that will by forfeiting the gift of salvation. *"Once saved, always saved"* is a dangerous doctrine, which often results in a person casting off the responsibility of living a holy life before God. What often happens is that before long, sin creeps in and the person walks away from God altogether. It is true that we are saved because of Jesus' perfect righteousness, not our own, but regardless, when God saves us, He does not want us to live a life of sin (Romans 6: 14). He prefers to use us for the betterment of His Kingdom, as we share the Gospel with others.

When we make Jesus not only our Saviour, but also make Him the Lord of our lives, then we wholeheartedly yield our lives to God, for the glory of His Kingdom and to do His will on Earth. It is a complete denial of ourselves and requires *"a white funeral,"* when we die to self and are resurrected into the new creation which God desires.

Unfortunately, some people only want the "Jesus that saves," the "Jesus that heals," the "Jesus that delivers" or the "genie in a bottle Jesus," who will grant them their heart's desires. But, the same people do not want to be associated with the "crucified Jesus," the one who gave *all of Himself* so that we could have eternal life.

When the Israelites were preparing for the first Passover in Egypt, God instructed Moses to tell the Children of Israel in Exodus 12: 9-11, concerning the Passover lamb, **"Eat not of it raw, or sodden at all with water, but roast with fire: his head with his legs, and with the purtenance thereof. And you shall let nothing of it remain until the morning; and that which** remains of it until the morning you shall burn with fire... it is the Lord's Passover."

This shows that *all* of the spotless lamb, which represented Jesus in every way, was to be consumed, even the **"purtenance,"** which were the intestines. The intestines were washed and placed back inside of the animal before it was to be roasted. What does this mean for the believer today? We cannot only accept the aspects of Jesus that are pleasant, but we must also partake of *all of Jesus*, which means not separating Him from the Cross, no matter how wretched His death was and no matter how the rest of the world may perceive us.

The Cross represents the death of Jesus, but please remember that it also represents us dying to our old self, which was tainted with the sin nature. Our sins were buried in the tomb with Jesus and when He was resurrected three days later, we also were resurrected to **"newness of life** (Romans 6: 3-4)."** 2 Corinthians 5:17 says, **"Therefore if any man be in Christ, he is a new creature: old things are passed away; behold, all things are become anew."**

Make no mistake, denying the finished work of Jesus on the Cross or adding to His once and for all sacrifice is a grievous sin. It makes the difference between pleasing God with the correct object of faith, which gain us eternal life in Heaven, or on the other hand, disappointing God by rejecting the free gift that He offered for salvation in His only Son, Jesus Christ. No matter how "good" you may be, or how much money you give to charity, or how often you attend church, the works of the flesh **"cannot please God** (Romans 8: 8)"** and will not earn a single thing from Him.

Chapter Eighteen

THE TIES THAT BIND

As we come to the close of this book, let me make the obvious statement: *Religion puts a person under bondage, but Jesus Christ gives liberty and freedom.* John 8: 36 says, **"If the Son therefore shall make you free, you shall be free indeed."** Anyone who has accepted Jesus as Lord and as Saviour knows exactly what I am saying. There is a freedom that is indescribable and only a person bought with the blood of Jesus can truly understand.

It is hard to articulate, but it's as if thousands of pounds have been lifted off of your shoulders the moment you admit that you were born a sinner and understand that you cannot save yourself. Once you realize that the only way out of bondage is by accepting that Jesus took your place on the Cross and died for your sins, then you can almost feel those heavy iron chains breaking and hear them crashing to the ground!

Life through the eyes of a person who has been born again of the Spirit is like seeing for the first time. It is a glorious second chance at life. A life that was born into sin and bound for a sinner's Hell, prepared for Satan and his fallen angels, is traded for a life bound for the glories of Heaven, where **"God shall wipe away all tears from their eyes; and there shall be no more death, neither sorrow, nor crying, neither shall there be any more pain...** (Revelation 21: 4)"

Religion has nothing to offer but a long, mind-boggling list of rules, regulations, commandments, sacraments and doctrines of men. None of it is sanctioned by God, but is instead devised by fallen mortal men, who think that they can speak for God outside of what His Word already reveals. *The bondage of religion complicates the simple Gospel and abrogates the finished work of Jesus on the Cross.*

Satan has created so many false ways of salvation that it can be confusing for someone who is not grounded in the truth of the Bible. I fell into that category for thirty-two years, until the Holy Spirit began to deal with me concerning my eternal soul. When I gave in and admitted that I wanted to know the truth, God sent me to people that could show me in the Bible what I needed to know. This book is dedicated to those ladies, who, to this very day, still join me each week in a Bible study.

In the beginning of this book, a series of questions were posed. Let us look at these questions again and reveal the final conclusion for each one:

(1) *Who, in their right mind, would want to be in bondage?* The answer is that no one truly wants to be in bondage. Most people desire freedom.

(2) *What does the Bible say about religion and religious people?* The Bible rebukes religion and Jesus called the religious Jews: **"hypocrites," "the blind leading the blind," "a generation of vipers"** and **"whited sepulchers full of dead men's bones."**

(3) *Why does being a part of a religion make people feel good about themselves and their eternal standing with God?* Because the by-product of religion is self-righteousness and it makes a person feel like the works of the flesh have earned him something from God. This euphoric feeling is mistaken for God's approval.

(4) *What truly pleases God?* Faith in the finished work of Jesus Christ on the Cross, with nothing added and nothing taken away is the *only* thing that pleases God.

(5) *From where should we gather our beliefs?* From a word-for-word translation Bible, the written Word of God, which was inspired by the Holy Spirit and holds the answers to all of life's many questions.

(6) *Can a person earn something from God by good works and exemplary behavior?* Good works and exemplary behavior cannot earn us anything from God, but a person who is born again of the Spirit will perform good works and live a holy life with the right motives of furthering the Gospel for others to come into the Kingdom of God.

(7) *Will devoted religious people go to Heaven upon death?* Unfortunately, if someone's faith is in their church or religion and not in Jesus Christ's finished work on the Cross, then that person will not go to Heaven.

(8) *Can dedicated religious people go to Hell?* Again, as sad as this reality may be, devoted religious people can go to Hell because they have rejected Jesus' once and for all sacrifice for their sins and placed their faith in their own ability to save themselves by religious works.

The bondage of religion has condemned multitudes of people to Hell and that is why this book was written. Maybe it will keep one more soul from believing the lies of Satan and following their own heart or a man-made religion. The strait and narrow **"gate"** may not be the most attractive way and today's world may mock you for denying self and living for God as He desires, but the promises of Heaven outweigh anything that this world has to offer. In Luke 9: 24-25, Jesus says, **"For whosoever will save his life shall lose it: but whosoever will lose his life for My sake, the same shall save it. For what is a man advantaged, if he gain the whole world, and lose himself, or be cast away?"**

I would love to finish this book with some of the lyrics of a song called, *"Whenever I Hear His Name."* These anointed words are the anthem of this book:

To those who have not met the Saviour
To hear it as just one more name
To those who have not known its power
So often speak it in vain

But I know this Jesus who saved me one day
Now I hear His Name in a different way

I hear the sounding of CHAINS falling down
As another SLAVE walks away FREE
I hear the cry in the darkest of nights
As a VICTIM declares VICTORY

I hear a melody angels can sing
A chorus that rises from all the redeemed
Anthem of praise
The saints of all ages proclaim
That's what I hear, whenever I hear His Name
JESUS...

People who reject God's way sincerely believe that they have freedom and see those who believe the Bible as slaves, but it is actually the complete opposite. They are the ones in bondage and those who have accepted Jesus as Lord and Saviour have freedom. Let's look again at the synonyms for the word "bondage:" *slavery, enslavement, servitude, subjugation, subjection, oppression, domination, exploitation.* Jesus is the *only one* who holds the key to unlock that iron padlock on the front cover of this book. Once you allow him to do that for you, the chains of bondage will come falling down and you can walk away free.

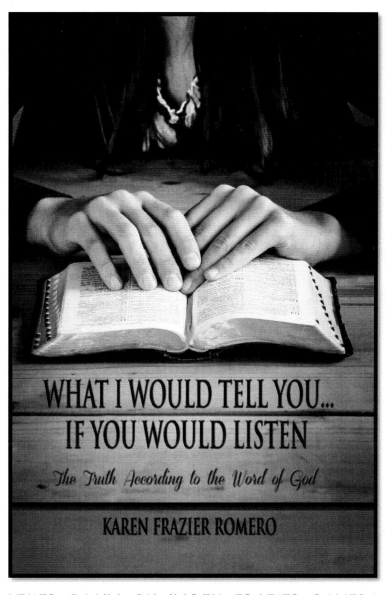

OTHER BOOKS BY KAREN FRAZIER ROMERO
AVAILABLE ON AMAZON.COM

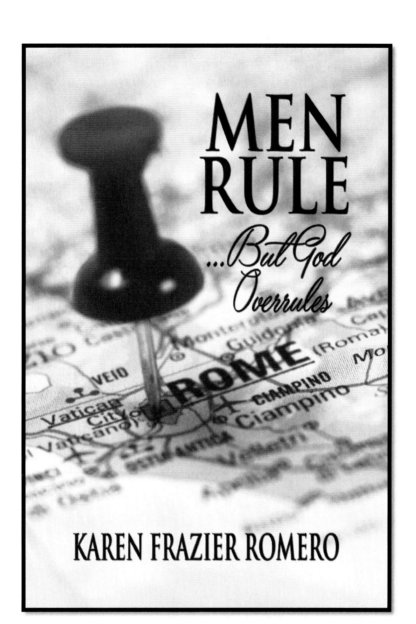

MEN RULE
...But God Overrules

KAREN FRAZIER ROMERO

WHILE MEN SLEPT...

...his enemy came and sowed tares among the wheat
MATTHEW 13:25

KAREN FRAZIER ROMERO

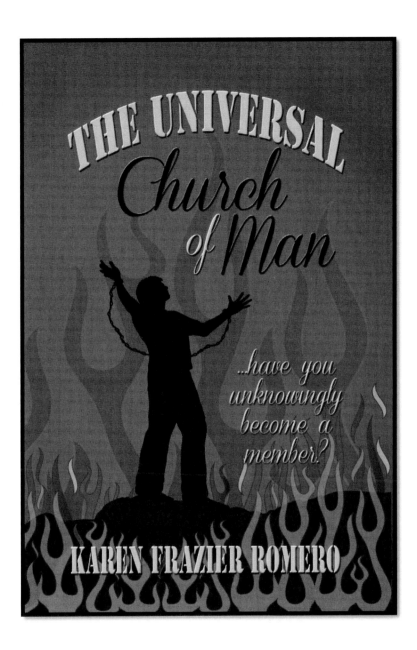

THE UNIVERSAL Church of Man

...have you unknowingly become a member?

KAREN FRAZIER ROMERO

THE
BROAD

and

NARROW
WAY

One soul on two different paths to eternity

KAREN FRAZIER ROMERO

TAKING THE

Bait

Unity

KAREN FRAZIER ROMERO